EX LIBRIS

VINTAGE CLASSICS

Virginia Woolf was born in London in 1882, the daughter of Sir Leslie Stephen, first editor of *The Dictionary of National Biography*. After his death in 1904 Virginia and her sister, the painter Vanessa Bell, moved to Bloomsbury and became the centre of 'The Bloomsbury Group'. This informal collective of artists and writers, which included Lytton Strachey and Roger Fry, exerted a powerful influence over early twentieth-century British culture.

In 1912 Virginia married Leonard Woolf, a writer and social reformer. Three years later, her first novel *The Voyage Out* was published, followed by *Night and Day* (1919) and *Jacob's Room* (1922). These first novels show the development of Virginia Woolf's distinctive and innovative narrative style. It was during this time that she and Leonard Woolf founded The Hogarth Press with the publication of the co-authored *Two Stories* in 1917, hand-printed in the dining room of their house in Surrey. The majority of Virginia Woolf's work was first published by The Hogarth Press, and these original texts are now available, together with her selected letters and diaries, from Vintage Classics, which belongs to the publishing group that Hogarth became part of in 1987.

Between 1925 and 1931 Virginia Woolf produced what are now regarded as her finest masterpieces, from *Mrs Dalloway* (1925) to the poetic and highly experimental novel *The Waves* (1931). She also maintained an astonishing output of literary criticism, short fiction, journalism and biography, including the playfully subversive *Orlando* (1928) and *A Room of One's Own* (1929), a passionate feminist essay. This intense creative productivity was often matched by periods of mental illness, from which she had suffered since her mother's death in 1895. On 28 March 1941, a few months before the publication of her final novel, *Between the Acts*, Virginia Woolf committed suicide.

Stuart N. Clarke has edited the *Virginia Woolf Bulletin* of the Virginia Woolf Society since its first number in 1999, and has edited volumes 5 and 6 of *The Essays of Virginia Woolf* for The Hogarth Press.

ALSO BY VIRGINIA WOOLF

Novels

The Voyage Out

Night and Day

The Years

Mrs Dalloway

To the Lighthouse

Orlando

The Waves

Between the Acts

The Years

Shorter Fiction

The Haunted House: The Complete Shorter Fiction

Non-Fiction and Other Works

Flush

Roger Fry

A Room of One's Own and *Three Guineas*

The Common Reader Vols 1 and 2

Selected Diaries (edited by Anne Oliver Bell)

Selected Letters (edited by Joanne Trautmann Banks)

VIRGINIA WOOLF

Street Haunting and Other Essays

EDITED WITH AN INTRODUCTION BY
Stuart N. Clarke

VINTAGE BOOKS
London

Published by Vintage 2014

Introduction and editorial notes © Stuart N. Clarke, 2014

Vintage
Random House, 20 Vauxhall Bridge Road,
London SW1V 2SA

www.vintage-classics.info

Addresses for companies within The Random House Group Limited
can be found at: www.randomhouse.co.uk/offices.htm

The Random House Group Limited Reg. No. 954009

A CIP catalogue record for this book
is available from the British Library

ISBN 9780099589778

The Random House Group Limited supports the Forest Stewardship
Council® (FSC®), the leading international forest-certification
organisation. Our books carrying the FSC label are printed on
FSC®-certified paper. FSC is the only forest-certification scheme
supported by the leading environmental organisations, including
Greenpeace. Our paper procurement policy can be found at:
www.randomhouse.co.uk/environment

Printed and bound in Great Britain by
Clays Ltd, St Ives plc

CONTENTS

Lives of the Obscure

Education

Places

INTRODUCTION
by Stuart N. Clarke

Virginia Woolf served a long literary apprenticeship. Shortly after her father died in 1904, she started writing reviews for the *Guardian*, a Church of England weekly of considerable influence in the nineteenth century but then in decline. She gradually moved her allegiance to the *Times Literary Supplement*, which had only been founded in 1902, and she remained loyal to it (with decreasing enthusiasm) until its editor Bruce Richmond retired at the end of 1937. Both journals published reviews anonymously and one might have thought that this allowed its contributors greater freedom. In fact, it did not, because the reviews were in effect the mouthpiece of each journal. Of course, as she began to write for other journals and gained in confidence, in time she found that she could allow herself to wander from the restrictions of the book under review.

When Woolf's husband Leonard became literary editor of the *Nation and the Athenaeum* in 1923, she gained an additional freedom, and for it she wrote signed reviews, short unsigned reviews, and even occasional anonymous one-paragraph contributions to miscellaneous columns, such as the following:

> Can neither war nor peace teach the French to translate or even to spell English? Glancing through a catalogue of pictures the other day which was thoughtfully provided with translations into English and German, I came upon 'Le Dessert' translated 'Leavings', 'Le torso d'une jeune femme' translated 'Young woman's trunk', and so on and so on. No English proof-reader would dare pass such misquotations of Racine as we put up with whenever Shakespeare is quoted in French. But there is a charm in the arrogance of French illiteracy, which takes it for granted that all languages save one are the base dialects of savages.[1]

Nevertheless, Woolf remained worried by the formal literary manner of many of her essays:

> the Victorian manner is perhaps – I am not sure – a disadvantage in writing. When I read my old *Literary Supplement* articles, I lay the blame for their suavity, their politeness, their sidelong approach, to my tea-table training. I see myself, not reviewing a book, but handing plates of buns to shy young men and asking them: do they take cream and sugar? On the other hand, the surface manner allows one, as I have found, to slip in things that would be inaudible if one marched straight up and spoke out loud.[2]

Woolf's 'sidelong approach' and frequent irony gave her the means to slip controversial subject matter into her novel *Orlando* (1928) and it (just) passed the censors, while Radclyffe Hall's contemporaneous *The Well of Loneliness* was banned.

Woolf never wrote a slashing review, so it is rare for her to write something as direct as: 'We are nauseated by the sight of trivial personalities decomposing in the eternity of print.'[3] Although she was a generous reviewer, one book was to her so entertainingly bad that she was able to produce three reviews of it: for the *TLS*, the *Daily Herald* and the *Athenaeum*. This was of Constance Hill's *Mary Russell Mitford and Her Surroundings* (1920). It is obviously the kind of book that goes in for: 'as we looked upon the steps leading down from the upper room, we fancied that we saw the tiny figure jumping from step to step'. Woolf pretends to puzzle over why Miss Hill chose to write about Miss Mitford, and concludes: 'In the first place, Miss Mitford was a lady; in the second, she was born in the year 1787 . . . Surroundings, as they are called, are invariably eighteenth-century surroundings.' Despite Miss Mitford's respectability, she had a father – 'terrible to relate' – an appalling, 'gluttonous, bibulous, amorous old man'. Woolf sums up: 'That is the worst of writing about ladies; they have fathers as well as teapots.'

In various incarnations and editions *The Week-End Book* has rarely been out of print since its initial appearance in 1924. Woolf thought little of it and her review is written in the form of a description of a country-house party where the guests bicker about the book. She ends with enthusiasm for nature and the great outdoors: 'what did we like, as we trooped . . . out of doors? Everything in the whole world . . . but not, we agreed, as we rambled off into the vast and glorious freedom of the universe, that book.'

Woolf's irony ranges from the simple to the subtle. In 'Trousers', Woolf confesses that she is unable to grasp the author's thesis, 'Owing to native obtuseness, no doubt'. We have no doubts either: of course Woolf is *not* obtuse. On the other hand, it is easy to read 'Middlebrow' as an essay purely about class, with Woolf as a representative of the upper classes praising the working classes while despising the middle classes. Instead, she is challenging the assumption that high-, middle- and lowbrow correspond to those three classes.[4] She is careful to point out: 'I myself have known duchesses who were highbrows, also charwomen'. In 'Thunder at Wembley' it is the British Empire and the mediocrity of its Exhibition she is criticising, by pricing everything at six and eightpence (one-third of £1): 'Dress fabrics, rope, table linen, old masters, sugar, wheat, filigree silver, pepper, birds' nests (edible, and exported to Hong-Kong), camphor, bees-wax, rattans, and the rest – why trouble to ask the price? One knows beforehand – six and eightpence.' She does not jeer at the visitors, who have a 'dignity of their own', even when clustered around a model of 'the Prince of Wales in butter' (she kids you not).

Those who may have struggled with Woolf's modernist novels – *Jacob's Room*, *Mrs Dalloway*, *To the Lighthouse*, *The Waves* – will perhaps be surprised by the pellucid prose of Woolf's essays. In them there is none of the affected style that will sometimes be found in the writings of Edith Sitwell and Rose Macaulay. In her novels, Woolf needed to find a form that would express her vision. As she wrote about *Mrs Dalloway*, 'it was necessary to write the book first and to invent a theory afterwards'. [5] By contrast, her essays are immediately accessible, and she refused to write for avant-garde magazines with a specific artistic or political slant. She 'fought shy of magazines which have a declared character. Why lay down laws about imaginative writing?'[6] It has been said that she 'was arguably the last of the great English essayists'.[7] A reviewer wrote in 1932 that 'most readers . . . will be enchanted . . . whether or not they have read what she is writing about . . . When a great novelist brings to the study of fact the qualities that give her such authority in fiction, lovers of fact must be grateful'.[8] He was reviewing *The Common Reader: Second Series*, which contains distinguished essays on *The Countess of Pembroke's Arcadia*, Donne, *Robinson Crusoe*, Swift's *Journal to Stella*, Sterne's *A Sentimental Journey*, among many others. Quentin Bell wrote that in Woolf's 'critical works one can sometimes hear her voice, but it is always a little formal, a little editorial'.[9] *The Common Reader: Second Series* deals with few contemporary authors, and only one essay from it, 'The Niece of an Earl', is included below.

Virginia Woolf is popularly perceived as remote, chilly and austere. So powerful is this image that even her spoof biography *Orlando* is sometimes seen as an aberration. Yet she wrote in her diary about it: 'I want fun. I want fantasy. I want (& this was serious) to give things their caricature value.'[10] While some critics have even taken seriously her preface to the book, her friend Raymond Mortimer, who is among those listed in it, was one of the first to describe *Orlando* as a 'lark': 'The preface is a parody of prefaces and the whole book is written in tearing high spirits'.[11] Her friends and family took this aspect of Woolf for granted. Vita Sackville-West's younger son Nigel Nicolson remembered that 'when she was coming to stay . . . Our immediate reaction was "Oh, good."' Her nephews and niece reacted similarly: 'Everybody said, "Oh, hooray, Virginia's coming to tea. Now we shall enjoy ourselves." Because she was very enlivening and spiriting.'[12] Her effect on adults was similar. Her brother-in-law Clive Bell recalled

some dark, uneasy, winter days during the first war in the depth of the country with Lytton Strachey. After lunch, as we watched the rain pour down and premature darkness roll up, he said, in his personal, searching way, 'Loves apart, whom would you most like to see coming up the drive?' I hesitated a moment, and he supplied the answer: 'Virginia of course.'[13]

If you read Woolf's *Selected Letters* (also published by Vintage), you will get some idea of the enlivening personality that her family and friends experienced. Of her books, the one that most closely expresses her personality is *A Room of One's Own*. Her nephew and biographer Quentin Bell tells us that there 'one hears Virginia speaking . . . she gets very close to her conversational style'.[14] When she contrasts the luxury of the men's colleges with the poverty of the women's in *A Room of One's Own*, she compares two meals: lunch in a men's college with 'partridges, many and various, [that] came with all their retinue of sauces and salads', while dinner at a women's college has only 'beef with its attendant greens and potatoes – a homely trinity, suggesting the rumps of cattle in a muddy market'. The dinner ends with biscuits and cheese: 'here the water-jug was liberally passed round, for it is the nature of biscuits to be dry, and these were biscuits to the core'.[15]

But there are streaks of humour, wit and above all irony that run through all of Woolf's writings, and we smile along with her. Here, for example, she slips this little remark into a review: 'In England the atmosphere is naturally aqueous, and as if there weren't enough outside, we drench ourselves with tea and coffee at least four times a day.'[16] In 'America, which I Have Never Seen . . .', she imagines a country that she would never visit:

'The Americans never sit down to a square meal. They perch on steel stools and take what they want from a perambulating rail. The Americans have swallowed their dinner by the time it takes us to decide whether the widow of a general takes precedence of the wife of a knight commander of the Star of India.'

Most of the essays in this collection are fairly informal, and they were chosen with the principal intention of entertaining the reader. But, just as in that quotation from 'America, which I Have Never Seen . . .', where there is an implied criticism of the British class system, behind the humour is Woolf's consistent view of the world: that books should be well written; that the British Empire, the class system and the patriarchy oppress; and that individuals have an intrinsic interest of their own.

The essays below have been allocated to somewhat arbitrary categories, including reviews of books she considered second-rate (although sometimes it is the subjects of the books that are second-rate) and critiques of Empire and of the class system. There is a section on the lives of the obscure: 'one likes romantically to feel oneself a deliverer advancing with lights across the waste of years to the rescue of some stranded ghost'.[17] Woolf read all sorts of biographies by all sorts of people. Who would have expected her to have read By Guess and by God, which she calls 'a very exciting yet infinitely childish book' and which turns out to have been about the author's experiences in the submarine fleet in the First World War? In reality she was so far removed from the fabled ivory tower that she always wanted to know what it was like – 'being a conductor, being a woman with ten children and thirty-five shillings a week, being a stockbroker, being an admiral, being a bank clerk, being a dressmaker, being a duchess, being a miner, being a cook, being a prostitute'.

In the education section, Woolf touches on class, money, privilege, and women's (lack of) education. The jokes in *A Room of One's Own* were not just jests. Woolf exaggerates the differences between the men's and women's colleges so that the narrator (and the reader) will question: 'Why did men drink wine and women water? Why was one sex so prosperous and the other so poor?'

Finally, there is a disparate group of essays on places, ending with one of Woolf's best and longest essays, 'Street Haunting: A London Adventure'. Evocative and indeed haunting – how can we explain the significance of 'the story of the dwarf, of the blind men, of the party in the Mayfair mansion, of the quarrel in the stationer's shop'? Here we find her writing the pure essay: 'The principle which controls it is simply that it should give pleasure'. It 'must lap us about and draw its curtain across the world'.[18] In 'Street Haunting' Woolf walks us around her patch of London, introducing us to some of its denizens: fascinating, unthreatening, but ultimately mysterious. Like Woolf herself. She is the guide at our shoulder, but perhaps we also glimpse her suddenly at a distance:

> the firelight wavers and the lamplight falls upon the privacy
> of some drawing-room, its easy chairs, its papers, its china,
> its inlaid table, and the figure of a woman, accurately
> measuring out the precise number of spoons of tea which
> – She looks at the door as if she heard a ring downstairs
> and somebody asking, is she in?

1–An untitled paragraph in the 'From Alpha to Omega' column signed 'Omicron' in the *Nation and the Athenaeum*, 22 November 1924. It was introduced by 'A correspondent writes:'. The offending catalogue has not been identified, but it is likely to have had *torse*, the French for *torso*. The paragraph is reprinted in *The Essays of Virginia Woolf*,Vol. 3, ed. Andrew McNeillie (Hogarth Press, 1988), p. 459.

2–*Moments of Being* (Pimlico, 2002), p. 152.

3–'The Modern Essay' in *The Common Reader* (Vintage 2003), p. 217.

4–See Melba Cuddy-Keane, 'Brow-Beating, Wool-Gathering, and the Brain of the Common Reader' in *Virginia Woolf Out of Bounds: Selected Papers from the Tenth Annual Conference on Virginia Woolf*, ed. Jessica Berman and Jane Goldman (Pace University Press, 2001), pp. 58–66.

5–*The Essays of Virginia Woolf*, Vol. 4, ed. Andrew McNeillie (Hogarth Press, 1994), p. 550.

6–*The Letters of Virginia Woolf*,Vol. 6, ed. Nigel Nicolson (Hogarth Press, 1980), p. 252.

7–Introduction, *The Essays of Virginia Woolf*, Vol. 1, ed. Andrew McNeillie (Hogarth Press, 1986), p. ix.

8–Quoted in *The Essays of Virginia Woolf*, Vol. 6, ed. Stuart N. Clarke (Hogarth Press, 2011), p. 477 n2.

9–Quentin Bell, *Virginia Woolf: A Biography* (Pimlico, 1996), p. 144 in vol. 2.

10–*The Diary of Virginia Woolf*,Vol. 3, ed. Anne Olivier Bell (Hogarth Press, 1980), p. 203.

11–Raymond Mortimer, 'Mrs. Woolf and Mr. Strachey', *Bookman* (New York), February 1929, p. 628, reprinted in *Virginia Woolf: The Critical Heritage*, ed. Robin Majumdar and Allen McLaurin (Routledge, 1975), p. 241.

12–'The Mind and Times of Virginia Woolf' (from 16' 44"), additional feature (2003) on *The Hours* DVD (Z1 D888844).

13–Clive Bell, *Old Friends* (Chatto & Windus, 1956), p. 118.

14–*Virginia Woolf: A Biography* p. 144 in vol. 2.

15–'*A Room of One's Own' and 'Three Guineas'* (Vintage, 1996), pp. 10, 16, 17.

16–'A Talk about Memoirs', *The Essays of Virginia Woolf*,Vol. 3, p. 181.

17–'Taylors and Edgeworths', *The Essays of Virginia Woolf*,Vol. 4, p. 119.

18–'The Modern Essay', p. 211.

The Common Reader

There is a sentence in Dr Johnson's Life of Gray which might well be written up in all those rooms, too humble to be called libraries, yet full of books, where the pursuit of reading is carried on by private people. '. . . I rejoice to concur with the common reader; for by the common sense of readers, uncorrupted by literary prejudices, after all the refinements of subtilty and the dogmatism of learning, must be finally decided all claim to poetical honours.' It defines their qualities; it dignifies their aims; it bestows upon a pursuit which devours a great deal of time, and is yet apt to leave behind it nothing very substantial, the sanction of the great man's approval.

The common reader, as Dr Johnson implies, differs from the critic and the scholar. He is worse educated, and nature has not gifted him so generously. He reads for his own pleasure rather than to impart knowledge or correct the opinions of others. Above all, he is guided by an instinct to create for himself, out of whatever odds and ends he can come by, some kind of whole – a portrait of a man, a sketch of an age, a theory of the art of writing. He never ceases, as he reads, to run up some rickety and ramshackle fabric which shall give him the temporary satisfaction of looking sufficiently like the real object to allow of affection, laughter, and argument. Hasty, inaccurate, and superficial, snatching now this poem, now that scrap of old furniture, without caring where he finds it or of what nature it may be so long as it serves his purpose and rounds his structure, his deficiencies as a critic are too obvious to be pointed out; but if he has, as Dr Johnson maintained, some say in the final distribution of poetical honours, then, perhaps, it may be worth while to write down a few of the ideas and opinions which, insignificant in themselves, yet contribute to so mighty a result.

Bad Books

The Anatomy of Fiction

Sometimes at country fairs you may have seen a professor on a platform exhorting the peasants to come up and buy his wonder-working pills. Whatever their disease, whether of body or mind, he has a name for it and a cure; and if they hang back in doubt he whips out a diagram and points with a stick at different parts of the human anatomy, and gabbles so quickly such long Latin words that first one shyly stumbles forward and then another, and takes his bolus and carries it away and unwraps it secretly and swallows it in hope. 'The young aspirant to the art of fiction who knows himself to be an incipient realist', Mr Hamilton vociferates from his platform, and the incipient realists advance and receive – for the professor is generous – five pills together with nine suggestions for home treatment. In other words they are given five 'review questions' to answer, and are advised to read nine books or parts of books, '1. Define the difference between realism and romance. 2. What are the advantages and disadvantages of the realistic method? 3. What are the advantages and disadvantages of the romantic method?' – that is the kind of thing they work out at home, and with such success that a 'revised and enlarged edition' of the book has been issued on the tenth anniversary of the first publication. In America, evidently, Mr Hamilton is considered a very good

5

professor, and has no doubt a bundle of testimonials to the miraculous nature of his cures. But let us consider: Mr Hamilton is not a professor; we are not credulous plough-boys; and fiction is not a disease.

In England we have been in the habit of saying that fiction is an art. We are not taught to write novels; dissuasion is our most usual incentive; and though perhaps the critics have 'deduced and formulated the general principles of the art of fiction', they have done their work as a good housemaid does hers; they have tidied up after the party is over. Criticism seldom or never applies to the problems of the present moment. On the other hand, any good novelist, whether he be dead or alive, has something to say about them, though it is said very indirectly, differently to different people, and differently at different stages of the same person's development. Thus, if anything is essential, it is essential to do your reading with your own eyes. But, to tell the truth, Mr Hamilton has sickened us of the didactic style. Nothing appears to be essential save perhaps an elementary knowledge of the A.B.C., and it is pleasant to remember that Henry James, when he took to dictation, dispensed even with that. Still, if you have a natural taste for books it is probable that after reading *Emma*, to take an instance, some reflections upon the art of Jane Austen may occur to you – how exquisitely one incident relieves another; how definitely, by not saying something, she says it; how surprising, there-fore, her expressive phrases when they come. Between the sentences, apart from the story, a little shape of some kind builds itself up. But learning from books is a capricious business at best, and the teaching so vague and changeable that in the end, far from calling books either 'romantic' or 'realistic', you will be more inclined to think them, as you think people, very mixed, very distinct, very unlike one another. But this would never do for Mr Hamilton. According to him every work of art can be taken to pieces, and those pieces can be named and numbered, divided and sub-divided, and given their order of precedence, like the internal organs of a frog. Thus we learn how to put them together again – that is, according to Mr Hamilton, we learn how to write. There is the complication, the major knot, and the explication; the inductive and the deductive methods; the kinetic and the static; the direct and the indirect with sub-divisions of the same; connotation, annotation, personal equation, and denotation; logical sequence and chronological succession – all parts of the frog and all capable of further dissection. Take the case of 'emphasis' alone. There are eleven kinds of emphasis. Emphasis by terminal position, by initial position, by pause, by direct proportion, by inverse proportion, by iteration, by antithesis, by surprise, by suspense – are you tired already? But consider the Americans. They have written one story eleven times over, with a different kind of emphasis in each. Indeed, Mr Hamilton's book teaches us a great deal about the Americans.

Still, as Mr Hamilton uneasily perceives now and then, you may dissect your frog, but you cannot make it hop; there is, unfortunately, such a thing as life. Directions for imparting life to fiction are given, such as to 'train yourself rigorously never to be bored', and to cultivate 'a lively curiosity and a ready sympathy'. But it is evident that Mr Hamilton does not like life, and, with such a tidy museum as his, who can blame him? He has found life very troublesome, and, if you come to consider it, rather unnecessary; for, after all, there are books. But Mr Hamilton's views on life are so illuminating that they must be given in his own words:

Perhaps in the actual world we should never bother to converse with illiterate provincial people; and yet we do not feel it a waste of time and energy to meet them in the pages of *Middlemarch*. For my own part, I have always, in actual life, avoided meeting the sort of people that appear in Thackeray's *Vanity Fair*, and yet I find it not only interesting but profitable to associate with them through the entire extent of a rather lengthy novel. 'Illiterate provincial people' – 'interesting but profitable' – 'waste of time and energy' – now after much wandering and painful toil we are on the right track at last. For long it seemed that nothing could reward the American people for having written eleven themes upon the eleven kinds of emphasis. But now we perceive dimly that there is something to be gained by the daily flagellation of the exhausted brain. It is not a title; it has nothing to do with pleasure or with literature; but it appears that Mr Hamilton and his industrious band see far off upon the horizon a circle of superior enlightenment to which, if only they can keep on reading long enough, they may attain. Every book demolished is a milestone passed. Books in foreign languages count twice over. And a book like this is of the nature of a dissertation to be sent up to the supreme examiner, who may be, for anything we know, the ghost of Matthew Arnold. Will Mr Hamilton be admitted? Can they have the heart to reject anyone so ardent, so dusty, so worthy, so out of breath? Alas! look at his quotations; consider his comments upon them:

'The murmuring of innumerable bees' . . . The word innumerable, which denotes to the intellect merely 'incapable of being numbered,' is, in this connection, made to suggest to the senses the murmuring of bees.

The credulous ploughboy could have told him more than that. It is not necessary to quote what he says about 'magic casements' and the 'iniquity of oblivion'. Is there not, upon page 208, a definition of style?

No; Mr Hamilton will never be admitted; he and his disciples must toil for ever in the desert sand, and the circle of illumination will, we fear, grow fainter and farther upon their horizon. It is curious to find, after writing the above sentence, how little one is ashamed of being, where literature is concerned, an unmitigated snob.

Wilcoxiana

How can one begin? Where can one leave off? There never was a more difficult book to review. If one puts in the Madame de Staël of Milwaukee, there will be no room for the tea-leaves; if one concentrates upon Helen Pitkin, Ralcey Husted Bell must be done without. Then all the time there are at least three worlds spinning in and out, and as for Ella Wheeler Wilcox – Mrs Wilcox is indeed the chief problem. It would be easy to make fun of her; equally easy to condescend to her; but it is not at all easy to express what one does feel for her. There is a hint of this complexity in her personal appearance. We write with forty photographs of Mrs Wilcox in front of us. If you omit those with the cats in her arms and the crescent moons in her hair, those stretched on a couch with a book, and those seated on a balustrade between Theodosia Garrison and Rhoda Hero Dunn, all primarily a tribute to the Muse, there remain a number which represent a plump, personable, determined young woman, vain, but extremely vivacious, arch, but at the same time sensible, and always in splendid health. She was never a frump at any stage of her career. Rather than look like a bluestocking, she would have forsaken literature altogether. She stuck a rod between her arms to keep her back straight; she galloped over the country on an old farm horse; she defied her mother and bathed naked; at the height of her fame 'a new stroke in swimming or a new high dive gave me more of a thrill than a new style of verse, great as my devotion to the Muses was, and ever has been'. In short, if one had the pleasure of meeting Mrs Wilcox, one would find her a very well-dressed, vivacious, woman of the world. But, alas for the simplicity of the problem! there is not one world but three.

The pre-natal world is indicated rather sketchily. One is given to understand that Mrs Wilcox is appearing for by no means the first time. There have been Ella Wheeler Wilcoxes in Athens and Florence, Rome and Byzantium. She is a recurring, but an improving phenomenon. 'Being an old soul myself,' she says, 'reincarnated many more times than any other member of my family, I knew the truth of spiritual things not revealed to them.' One gift, at least, of supreme importance she brought with her from the shades – 'I was born with unquenchable hope . . . I always expected wonderful things to happen to me.' Without hope, what could she have done? Everything was against her. Her father was an unsuccessful farmer; her mother an embittered woman worn down by a life of child-bearing and hard work; the atmosphere of the home was one of 'discontent and fatigue and irritability'. They lived far out in the country, five miles from a post office, uncomfortably remote even from the dissipations of Milwaukee. Yet Ella Wheeler never lost her belief in an amazing future before her; she was probably never dull for five minutes together. Although acutely aware that her father's taste in hats was distressing, and that the farmhouse walls were without creepers, she had the power within her to transform everything to an object of beauty. The buttercups and daisies of the fields looked to her like rare orchids and hothouse roses. When she was galloping to the post on her farm horse, she expected to be thrown at the feet of a knight, or perhaps the miracle would be reversed and it was into her bosom that the knight would be pitched instead. After a day of domestic drudgery, she would climb a little hill and sit in the sunset and dream. Fame was to come from the East, and love and wealth. (As a matter of fact, she notes, they came from the West.) At any rate something wonderful was bound to happen. 'And I would awaken happy in spite of myself, and put all my previous melancholy into verses – and dollars.' The young woman with the determined mouth never forgot her dollars, and one respects her for saying so. But often Miss Wheeler suggested that in return for what he called her 'heart wails' the editor should send her some object from his prize list – bric-à-brac, tableware, pictures – anything to make the farmhouse more like the house of her dreams. Among the rest came six silver forks, and, judge of her emotion! conceive the immeasurable romance of the world! – years later she discovered that the silver forks were made by the firm in which her husband was employed. But it is time to say something of the poetic gift which brought silver forks from Milwaukee, and letters and visits from complete strangers, so that she cannot remember 'any period of my existence when I have not been before the public eye'. She was taught very little; there were odd volumes of Shakespeare, Ouida, and Gauthier [sic] scattered about the house, but no complete sets. She did not wish to read, however. Her passion for writing seems to have been a natural instinct – a gift handed down mature from Heaven, and manifesting itself whenever it chose, without much control or direction from Mrs Wilcox herself. Sometimes the Muse would rise to meet an emergency. 'Fetch me a pencil and pad!' she would say, and, in the midst of a crowd, to the amazement of the beholders, and to the universal applause, she would dash off precisely the verse required to celebrate the unexpected arrival of General Sherman. Yet sometimes the Muse would obstinately forsake her. What could have been more vexatious than its behaviour in the Hotel Cecil, when Mrs Wilcox wished to write a poem about Queen Victoria's funeral? She had been sent across the Atlantic for that very purpose. Not a word could she write. The newspaperman was coming for her copy at nine the next morning. She had not put pen to paper when she went to bed. She was in despair. And then at the inconvenient hour of three a.m. the Muse relented. Mrs Wilcox woke with four verses running in her head. 'I felt an immense sense of relief. I knew I could write something the editor would like; something England would like.' And, indeed, 'The Queen's Last Ride' was set to music by a friend of King Edward's, and sung in the presence of the entire Royal family, one of whom afterwards graciously sent her a message of thanks.

Capricious and fanciful, nevertheless the Muse has a heart of gold; she never does desert Mrs Wilcox. Every experience turns, almost of its own accord and at the most unexpected moments, to verse. She goes to stay with friends; she sits next a young widow in the omnibus. She forgets all about it. But as she stands before the looking-glass fastening her white dress in the evening, something whispers to her:

> Laugh and the world laughs with you,
> Weep and you weep alone.
> For the sad old earth must borrow its mirth,
> It has trouble enough of its own.

The following morning at the breakfast table I recited the quatrain to the Judge and his wife . . . and the Judge, who was a great Shakespearean scholar, said, 'Ella, if you keep the remainder of the poem up to that epigrammatic standard, you will have a literary gem.'

She did keep the poem up to that standard, and two days later he said, 'Ella, that is one of the biggest things you ever did, and you are mistaken in thinking it uneven in merit, it is all good and up to the mark.' Such is the depravity of mankind, however, that a wretched creature called Joyce, belonging to 'the poison-insect order of humanity', as Mrs Wilcox says, afterwards claimed that he had written 'Solitude' himself – written it, too, upon the head of a whisky barrel in a wine-room.

A poetess also was very trying. Mrs Wilcox, who is generosity itself, detected unusual genius in her verse, and fell in love with the idea of playing Fairy Godmother to the provincial poetess. She invited her to stay at an hotel, and gave a party in her honour. Mrs Croly, Mrs Leslie, Robert Ingersoll, Nym Crinkle, and Harriet Webb all came in person. The carriages extended many blocks down the street. Several of the young woman's poems were recited; 'there was some good music and a tasteful supper'. Moreover, each guest, on leaving, was given a piece of ribbon upon which was printed the verse that Mrs Wilcox so much admired. What more could she have done? And yet the ungrateful creature went off with the barest words of thanks; scarcely answered letters; refused to explain her motives, and stayed in New York with an eminent literary man without letting Mrs Wilcox know.

To this day when I see the occasional gems of beauty which still fall from this poet's pen I feel the old wound ache in my heart . . . Life, however, always supplies a balm after

it has wounded us . . . The spring following this experience
my husband selected a larger apartment.

For by this time Ella Wheeler was Wilcox.

She first met Mr Wilcox in a jeweller's shop in Milwaukee.
He was engaged in the sterling-silver business, and she had
run to ask the time. Ironically enough, she never noticed
him. There was Mr Wilcox, a large, handsome man with
a Jewish face and a deep bass voice, doing business with the
jeweller, and she never noticed his presence. Out she went
again, anxious only to be in time for dinner, and thought
no more about it. A few days later a very distinguished-
looking letter arrived in a blue envelope. Might Mr Wilcox
be presented to her? 'I knew it was, according to established
ideas, bordering on impropriety, yet I so greatly admired
the penmanship and stationery of my would-be acquaintance
that I was curious to know more of him.' They corresponded.
Mr Wilcox's letters were 'sometimes a bit daring', but never
sentimental; and they were always enclosed in envelopes 'of
a very beautiful shade', while 'the crest on the paper seemed
to lead me away from everything banal and common'. And
then the Oriental paper-knife arrived. This had an
extraordinary effect upon her such as had hitherto been
produced only by reading 'a rare poem, or hearing lovely
music, or in the presence of some of Ouida's exotic
descriptions'. She went to Chicago and met Mr Wilcox in
the flesh. He seemed to her – correctly dressed and very
cultured in manner as he was – 'like a man from Mars'.
Soon afterwards they were married, and almost immediately
Mr Wilcox, to the profound joy of his wife, expressed his
belief in the immortality of the soul.

Mrs Wilcox was now established in New York, the
admired centre of a circle of 'very worth-while people'.

Her dreams in the sunset were very nearly realised. The Bungalow walls were covered with autographs of brilliant writers and the sketches of gifted artists. Universal brotherhood was attempted. It was the rule of the house 'to treat mendicants with sympathy and peddlers with respect'. No one left without 'some little feeling of uplift'. What was wanting? In the first place, 'the highbrows have never had any use for me.' The highbrows could be dispatched with a phrase. 'May you grow at least a sage bush of a heart to embellish your desert of intellect!'

All the same, in her next incarnation she will have nothing to do with genius. 'To be a gifted poet is a glory; to be a worth-while woman is a greater glory.' There are moments when she wishes that the Muse would leave her at peace. To be the involuntary mouthpiece of Songs of Purpose, Passion, and Power, greet the war with *Hello, Boys*, and death with *Sonnets of Sorrow and Triumph*, to feel that at any moment a new gem may form or a fresh cameo compose itself, what fate could be more appalling? Yet such has been the past, and such must be the future, of Ella Wheeler Wilcox.

Trousers

If the readers of the *New Statesman* will buy Mr Edwards'
book they will hear of something to their advantage. They
will learn that though they have always been accustomed
to think themselves average men they are, by reason of that
very fact, the only judges of art. Not only are they the only
judges, they are the only creators. For the average man can
cultivate his appearance, and that is the first of the arts; he
can behave like a gentleman, and that is the second; he can
dress well, and that is the third. The architect, the painter
and the sculptor, though admitted among the minor artists,
cannot compete with the man or woman who, divinely
beautiful, exquisitely tactful, and superbly attired, practises
the three major arts to perfection.

But our proficiency in the art of being beautiful is much
determined by the accidents of birth. At this point we find
Mr Edwards consoling, if not entirely convincing. 'Noses
straight, aquiline or retroussé may so harmoniously be set
upon the face that they are neither insignificant nor yet
obtrusive . . . One man may have rather thin legs, and
another man rather thick legs, and both may be possessed
of a good figure.' There is only one physical defect which
is completely damning, and that is bow legs. 'Bow legs are
an abomination. The reason is that, being arranged in two
equal and opposite curves enclosing a space, they create at

about the level of the knees where the space is widest a marked focal centre' – in short, the bow-legged are inevitably ill-bred; no one can help looking at their legs, and discord and rebellion result. The parents of the bow-legged, Mr Edwards is of opinion, 'ought to be visited with a severe penalty'.

Nevertheless, however scurvily Nature may have behaved, you can temper her severity (short of bow legs) by attention to the art of manners. Much can be done by grace of posture. You should be careful not to open the jaws widely, smack the lips, or expose the contents of the mouth in eating. Unless it is to amuse a baby, do not pretend to be a horse, for to walk on all fours 'without humorous intent' is to display 'the ultimate degree of bad manners to which it is possible to attain'.

But the shortest survey of Mr Edwards' book must not fail to point out that besides laying down the law the author is at great pains to ascertain what that law is. Owing to native obtuseness, no doubt, we have been unable to grasp the grammar of design, although Mr Edwards has been to Nature herself to discover it, and is confident that our assent will be complete and instantaneous 'because the law of mind has an intimate connection with the law of Nature, and it is impossible to acknowledge the one without paying an equal deference to the other'. In spite of diagrams of feet, hands, eyes, noses, ships and houses, many of his statements seem to us controversial, and some highly obscure. We will only mention the principle of resolved duality. 'Nature,' says Mr Edwards, 'does not tolerate duality.' The hands differ; so do the eyes. But when Mr Edwards goes on to assert that trousers, owing to 'the irremediable effect of duality', seem 'to invite disrespect', we entirely dissent. We go further. We have conceived them in isolation from the jacket, as advised, and still see nothing to laugh at in trousers. As for the final and most striking example of duality resolved, to wit, the Holy Trinity, the questions which Mr Edwards decides are too grave to be touched on in a review. We need only say that the origin of the Holy Ghost, long a subject of dispute among theologians, is now accounted for — quite simply, too.

A Letter to a Lady in Paraguay

. . . And the sun, you say, is almost too hot; the parrots wake you at dawn with their screeching, and it is only at sunset, when the horizon is all on fire with crimson dust, that you feel fresh again and bathe naked in a limpid, tepid, slightly swaying sea. One must believe a woman who has sat upon seven and sixty committees. But in return, how can I describe an English sick-room in February in London – the thermometer, the medicine glass, the bunch of insipid grapes, the six daffodils, and daylight drawing further and further its strip of elongated grey? 'The worst of it,' you go on, 'is that there are no books to read. The ants destroy them; no one has time to read them; and somehow one can't read a pocket Shakespeare in one's bedroom.' I have the better of you there. At a guess I should say that there are twenty-seven books on the table by my bedside – new books, old books, classics, ephemerals, biographies, novels, even poetry. I have tried them all and propose therefore in return for your sunsets and parrots to tell you about Mrs Barclay and Boswell and Princess Bibesco. Only you know what influenza is – how it smears the mind and disturbs the vision so that sometimes I am not sure whether I am reading or making up – whether Mrs Barclay is sitting in the arm-chair opposite or whether, with Princess Bibesco, I am drowsing in amber velvet among the poinsettias. Don't believe a word

I say, and for Heaven's sake don't pollute, even the South Americans, with my critical judgements.

I have lifted that phrase about the velvet and the poinsettias from the review of some rather sneering reviewer. Not one of them can take up his honest black pen without making it perfectly plain that amber velvet and poinsettias mean nothing to him; that he has never eaten off golden plate; worn golden slippers, or married a Prince; which, being set down at length, there is only room for a polite sneer at young women of 23 who have committed all these crimes and then have the impertinence to write stories. For my own part I was conscious of little except that the Princess put a hook in my nose and dragged me through some very stale and sultry waters in which I should otherwise have languished; and for this I can't help thanking her, be the risk what it may. Next time, if the Princess will be guided by me, she will leave out the love-letters, and print her pedigree instead. Stories by the granddaughter of a cobbler are sure, in our democracy, of the warmest welcome.

Mrs Barclay has the same initial as Princess Bibesco, and I turn therefore without more ado to consider her life by an anonymous, very straightforward, very simple-minded daughter. Now it would be easy to laugh at Mrs Barclay, and still easier, it appears (her books sell by the million in China and Japan) to take her seriously. What I want to do is to convey the impression that she was a gigantic humbug and at the same time a woman of genius. The brain was left out, but the driving power remained. She had the energy without the eye. This particular combination is not by any means remarkable – consider Garvice and Miss Corelli and Hall Caine and Ethel Dell and Mrs Wheeler Wilcox. They are the runaway motor-cars, the blazing timber-yards of modern literature, and to watch their speed and splendour and flame and extinction – and, after all, they never singe even a cat's whiskers – is one of the amusements of the age. But their biographies are better worth reading than their books. Here was Mrs Barclay (I cannot swear that I remember it all accurately), the daughter of one country clergyman and the wife of another. Nature had given her masses of curly hair, a splendid physique, a magnificent contralto voice. If a singer broke down she would take up his song and sing it straight through without a moment's hesitation until the hall rang with applause. She was utterly without shyness as she was entirely without conceit. Things happened like that – it was none of her doing. Almost automatically the ten village rustics who made up her first audience grew to a million Americans convulsed with one sob. If one had given her a melon seed over night it would have grown, one feels, into three pumpkins by the next morning. It was the same with her books. An attack of influenza, a prolonged convalescence, a half-sheet of notepaper, and *The Rosary* came into existence. No sooner begun than finished; no sooner finished than bound in purple; no sooner bound in purple than famous; and next year behold! the shores of America were purple in her honour, and reverend bald-headed gentlemen stood on the quayside waving purple banners inscribed with 'Welcome,' 'Barclay,' and 'Rosary.' Her single seed had grown into a million purple pumpkins.

This use of metaphor will not disguise from you the fact that I have not read a single page of any one of her books. Stay – I am exaggerating. One page is reproduced in this biography. The Lady Abbess leans from the convent window and reproaches Lord Hugh – there it ends. But I am sure that she was reproaching Lord Hugh for nothing more serious than the theft of a single rose. The page is a small one – I fancy she used the fly-sheets of her innumerable letters, and wrote as often as not in the train coming home from a meeting – the page is small, but enough to show me that I hate purple pumpkins more than any other of nature's products. They are squashy and fleshy and tasteless and sugary and tame. They go sour with extreme rapidity. Even the servants can't abide them after a time, and Heaven knows what finally becomes of them save that nature, I suppose, easily takes back into her bosom what that bosom so easily exudes. Her genius was nature's genius rather than man's – the genius which creates the cabbage and the dandelion and smothers all the hedgerows with foaming cow's parsley in June. But enough of these metaphors. To show you what I mean by calling Mrs Barclay a woman of genius I will tell you two anecdotes as accurately as I can. She had a passion for the poems of Mrs Browning (and parenthetically I may remark how odd it seems to me to think of Browning's chair or table in Mrs Barclay's boudoir). At Florence, of course, she sought out the grave of the poetess, and there she sat on a camp stool, took out her fountain pen, and wrote hour after hour, ream after ream. And then, of course, Americans collected. First they stared at Mrs Browning; then they stared at Mrs Barclay. 'What are you writing, if we may make so bold?' 'A novel.' 'And may we ask what novels you have written already?' A moment's hesitation, a smile, an arch glance, and then out it came: 'Well one of them was called *The Rosary*.' Consternations, exclamations, invitations! Was this really Mrs Barclay? Why, sister Ellen had died blessing her. Multiply this scene by a thousand at least. Set it in railway carriages, and omnibuses and mission-halls. Imagine cab-drivers and peeresses and prostitutes all kindling and stretching out their hands and never ceasing to bless the name of Mrs Barclay – well, what does one call the power that does all this but genius – allowing, of course, that it is genius without the brain. But the second anecdote is far more impressive. Mrs Barclay had only to dip her hand into the waters of Lake Windermere and shoals of minnows attached themselves to her finger-tips. This they did year after year in the presence of witnesses. Call it wizardry, or magnetism, or what you will, that is the power which sways multitudes, leads armies, and alters the destinies of nations. In a narrow sphere it keeps everything within ten miles of it on the boil, curls the hair, fires the eye, wakes up the countryside, and probably wears out its possessor long before Mr Conrad, for example, has written one whole page entirely to his liking.

There is another B on my list – Boswell; and how to connect him with Mrs Barclay on the inch of paper that remains to me I know not. The precipice is too steep, the problem too profound. For if you ask me which I prefer, Barclay or Boswell, life or literature, I shall have to turn on my pillow and think it out.

The Week End

This is a very prettily printed little book, with a gay dust cover, and a dull binding, and a book marker with 'Have you forgotten the salt?' on one side, and 'Have you forgotten the corkscrew?' on the other, and good poems and bad poems and games and songs and recipes and quips and cranks and blank pages for more games and songs and quips and cranks – in short, the very book to hand to one's hostess in return for a candlestick on Saturday night with a blessing. Instead of reviewing the book, it may be more to the point to describe simply what fruit that blessing bore on Sunday.

The day was hot; breakfast late. Through the half-open door a woman's voice could be heard reciting:

I scarcely believe my love to be so pure
As I had thought it was

– an embarrassing statement (since the book was forgotten), and matters were scarcely mended by the horrid agony of being forced to guess, on entering the room, who wrote it. Happily there was present a retired governor of one of our eastern possessions, who, taking the volume from her hand as she read on, cried out that, whoever wrote it, Donne did not. There was, it seems, an iniquitous misprint on that page; and under cover of his fulminations eating became momentarily feasible. A sunburnt egg might be hooked into proximity with a spoon. But could one eat it? The indefatigable woman was off again reciting Shakespeare, and the bold spirit has yet to be discovered who can crack an egg with intrepidity while Shakespeare is being read aloud. A tentative tapping came from some; others sat mute, bored, upright. However, the day was hot; the window open; the garden wide; escape possible. Roses, peonies, cauliflowers – we need not retail a list of garden produce at this season, nor make apology for that genial and pious spirit which, when the church bells ring to church, bids some of us resign ourselves to sleep. Only, the path was narrow; and people must walk up and down it two abreast. Even in the underworld of dreams it was impossible not to adumbrate some fantastic version of what the noise was all about. It was about poetry. First, that nobody could call that poetry; next, that everybody must admit this. Suddenly – and here the very dead must have wakened to see the wretched little book tossed and torn between a couple of infuriated readers – suddenly the word 'Emerson' rent the air. Emerson had been discovered among the laurels; couchant with Shelley and Keats; proclaimed by the anthologists the author of a 'great poem' – Emerson the American! Emerson the essayist! Worse was to come. A living rhymer, without even the varnish of death or antiquity to excuse the blasphemy, had intruded into the same holy spot. He too wrote 'great poems'. Since sleep was impossible, the morning might as well be wasted in argument; living against dead; classics against romantics; until the lunch bell rang, and dishevelled and bellicose the guests assembled to find their hostess, who had been to church, returned fresh for the pursuit. We were all to spend the afternoon, she said, playing games. *The Week-End Book*, of which she had regained possession, recommended Free Association Team Race, the Animal and the Stick Game, Famous People on Paper, Book Reviews, and many others. Moreover, it provided recipes for sandwiches and cocktails. She proposed to take us all for a walk and to wind up, as the kind people suggested, with a little music.

As she ended, animation was to be observed in some quarters. Upon others the shades of night descended. One of those deep and for the most part hidden abysses between man and man had been uncovered. Tempers would soon be lost. Thunder was brewing; satire preparing. The beef was getting cold; the servant maid was jogging people's elbows, when the old gentleman, who had ruled the East and subdued, no doubt, countless mutinies and hordes of wild elephants, observed that in his experience the race is divided thus: there are the sociables and there are the solitaries. One party, he said, is every bit as good as the other. (Tension relaxed.) Indeed, he said, each is indispensable to the other. (Amenity was restored.) Here we have an instance, he continued, pointing to the book. (Plates circulated.) The sociables, for whom this facetious and altogether well-meaning little book was written, are admirable citizens, people of spirit, adventure, and good will. Let them take their book, sing their songs, play their games, mix their cocktails, admire their poems, in company. Meanwhile the solitaries, to whom he owned that he belonged, will do, he said (and seldom has human face looked so divine), precisely what they like. And what did we like, as we trooped after him out of doors? Everything in the whole world. Pigs and calves; cocks and hens; the smell of beans and the smell of straw; roses and tobacco; but not, we agreed, as we rambled off into the vast and glorious freedom of the universe, that book.

Miss Mitford

Speaking truthfully, *Mary Russell Mitford and Her Surroundings* is not a good book. It neither enlarges the mind nor purifies the heart. There is nothing in it about Prime Ministers and not very much about Miss Mitford. Yet, as one is setting out to speak the truth, one must own that there are certain books which can be read without the mind and without the heart, but still with considerable enjoyment. To come to the point, the great merit of these scrapbooks, for they can scarcely be called biographies, is that they license mendacity. One cannot believe what Miss Hill says about Miss Mitford, and thus one is free to invent Miss Mitford for oneself. Not for a second do we accuse Miss Hill of telling lies. That infirmity is entirely ours. For example: 'Alresford was the birthplace of one who loved nature as few have loved her, and whose writings "breathe the air of the hayfields and the scent of the hawthorn boughs", and seem to waft to us "the sweet breezes that blow over ripened cornfields and daisied meadows".' It is perfectly true that Miss Mitford was born at Alresford, and yet, when it is put like that, we doubt whether she was ever born at all. Indeed she was, says Miss Hill; she was born 'on the 16th December 1787. "A pleasant house in truth it was," Miss Mitford writes. "The breakfast-room ... was a lofty and spacious apartment."' So Miss Mitford was born in the breakfast-room about eight-thirty on a snowy morning between the Doctor's second and third cups of tea. 'Pardon me,' said Mrs Mitford, turning a little pale, but not omitting to add the right quantity of cream to her husband's tea, 'I feel . . .' That is the way in which Mendacity begins. There is something plausible and even ingenious in her approaches. The touch about the cream, for instance, might be called historical, for it is well known that when Mary won £20,000 in the Irish lottery, the Doctor spent it all upon Wedgwood china, the winning number being stamped upon the soup plates in the middle of an Irish harp, the whole being surmounted by the Mitford arms, and encircled by the motto of Sir John Bertram, one of William the Conqueror's knights, from whom the Mitfords claimed descent. 'Observe,' says Mendacity, 'with what an air the Doctor drinks his tea, and how she, poor lady, contrives to curtsey as she leaves the room.' Tea? I inquire, for the Doctor, though a fine figure of a man, is already purple and profuse, and foams like a crimson cock over the frill of his fine laced shirt. 'Since the ladies have left the room,' Mendacity begins, and goes on to make up a pack of lies with the sole object of proving that Dr Mitford kept a mistress in the purlieus of Reading and paid her money on the pretence that he was investing it in a new method of lighting and heating houses invented by the Marquis de Chavannes. It came to the same thing in the end – to the King's Bench Prison, that is to say; but instead of allowing us to recall the literary and historical associations of the place, Mendacity wanders off to the window and distracts us again by the platitudinous remark that it is still snowing. There is something very charming in an ancient snowstorm. The weather has varied almost as much in the course of generations as mankind. The snow of those days was more formally shaped and a good deal softer than the snow of ours, just as an eighteenth-century cow was no more like our cows than she was like the florid and fiery cows of Elizabethan pastures. Sufficient attention has scarcely been paid to this aspect of literature, which, it cannot be denied, has its importance.

Our brilliant young men might do worse, when in search of a subject, than devote a year or two to cows in literature, snow in literature, the daisy in Chaucer and in Coventry Patmore. At any rate, the snow falls heavily. The Portsmouth mail-coach has already lost its way; several ships have foundered, and Margate pier has been totally destroyed. At Hatfield Peverel twenty sheep have been buried, and though one supports itself by gnawing wurzels which it has found near it, there is grave reason to fear that the French king's coach has been blocked on the road to Colchester. It is now the 16th of February 1808.

Poor Mrs Mitford! Twenty-one years ago she left the breakfast-room, and no news has yet been received of her child. Even Mendacity is a little ashamed of itself, and, picking up *Mary Russell Mitford and Her Surroundings*, assures us that everything will come right if we possess ourselves in patience. The French king's coach was on its way to Bocking; at Bocking lived Lord and Lady Charles Murray-Aynsley; and Lord Charles was shy. Lord Charles had always been shy. Once when Mary Mitford was five years old – sixteen years, that is, before the sheep were lost and the French king went to Bocking – Mary 'threw him into an agony of blushing by running up to his chair in mistake for that of my papa'. He had indeed to leave the room. Miss Hill, who, somewhat strangely, finds the society of Lord and Lady Charles pleasant, does not wish to quit it without 'introducing an incident in connection with them which took place in the month of February 1808'. But is

Miss Mitford concerned in it? we ask, for there must be an end of trifling. To some extent, that is to say, Lady Charles was a cousin of the Mitfords, and Lord Charles was shy. Mendacity is quite ready to deal with 'the incident' even on these terms; but, we repeat, we have had enough of trifling. Miss Mitford may not be a great woman; for all we know she was not even a good one; but we have certain responsibilities as a reviewer which we are not going to evade.

There is, to begin with, English literature. A sense of the beauty of Nature has never been altogether absent, however much the cow may change from age to age, from English poetry. Nevertheless, the difference between Pope and Wordsworth in this respect is very considerable. *Lyrical Ballads* was published in 1798; *Our Village* in 1824. One being in verse and the other in prose, it is not necessary to labour a comparison which contains, however, not only the elements of justice, but the seeds of many volumes. Like her great predecessor, Miss Mitford much preferred the country to the town; and thus, perhaps, it may not be inopportune to dwell for a moment upon the King of Saxony, Mary Anning, and the ichthyosaurus. Let alone the fact that Mary Anning and Mary Mitford had a Christian name in common, they are further connected by what can scarcely be called a fact, but may, without hazard, be called a probability. Miss Mitford was looking for fossils at Lyme Regis only fifteen years before Mary Anning found one. The King of Saxony visited Lyme in 1844, and seeing the head of an ichthyosaurus in Mary Anning's window, asked her to drive to Pinny and explore the rocks. While they were looking for fossils, an old woman seated herself in the King's coach – was she Mary Mitford? Truth compels us to say that she was not; but there is no doubt, and we are not trifling when we say it, that Mary Mitford often expressed a wish that she had known Mary Anning, and it is singularly unfortunate to have to state that she never did. For we have reached the year of 1844; Mary Mitford is fifty-seven years of age, and so far, thanks to Mendacity and its trifling ways, all we know of her is that she did not know Mary Anning, had not found an ichthyosaurus, had not been out in a snowstorm, and had not seen the King of France.

It is time to wring the creature's neck, and begin again at the very beginning.

What considerations, then, had weight with Miss Hill when she decided to write *Mary Russell Mitford and Her Surroundings*? Three emerge from the rest, and may be held of paramount importance. In the first place, Miss Mitford was a lady; in the second, she was born in the year 1787; and in the third, the stock of female characters who lend themselves to biographic treatment by their own sex is, for one reason or another, running short. For instance, little is known of Sappho, and that little is not wholly to her credit. Lady Jane Grey has merit, but is undeniably obscure. Of George Sand, the more we know the less we approve. George Eliot was led into evil ways which not all her philosophy can excuse. The Brontës, however highly we rate their genius, lacked that indefinable something which marks the lady; Harriet Martineau was an atheist; Mrs Browning was a married woman; Jane Austen, Fanny Burney, and Maria Edgeworth have been done already; so that, what with one thing and another, Mary Russell Mitford is the only woman left.

There is no need to labour the extreme importance of the date when we see the word 'surroundings' on the back of a book. Surroundings, as they are called, are invariably eighteenth-century surroundings. When we come, as of course we do, to that phrase which relates how 'as we looked upon the steps leading down from the upper room, we fancied we saw the tiny figure jumping from step to step', it would be the grossest outrage upon our sensibilities to be told that those steps were Athenian, Elizabethan, or Parisian. They were, of course, eighteenth-century steps, leading down from the old panelled room into the shady garden, where, tradition has it, William Pitt played marbles, or, if we like to be bold, where on still summer days we can almost fancy that we hear the drums of Bonaparte on the coast of France. Bonaparte is the limit of the imagination on one side, as Monmouth is on the other; it would be fatal if the imagination took to toying with Prince Albert or sporting with King John. But fancy knows her place, and there is no need to labour the point that her place is the eighteenth century. The other point is more obscure. One must be a lady. Yet what that means, and whether we like what it means, may both be doubtful. If we say that Jane Austen was a lady and that Charlotte Brontë was not one, we do as much as need be done in the way of definition, and commit ourselves to neither side.

It is undoubtedly because of their reticence that Miss Hill is on the side of the ladies. They sigh things off and they smile things off, but they never seize the silver table by the legs or dash the teacups on the floor. It is in many ways a great convenience to have a subject who can be trusted to live a long life without once raising her voice. Sixteen years is a considerable stretch of time, but of a lady it is enough to say, 'Here Mary Mitford passed sixteen years of her life and here she got to know and love not only their own beautiful grounds but also every turn of the surrounding shady lanes.' Her loves were vegetable, and her lanes were shady. Then, of course, she was educated at the school where Jane Austen and Mrs Sherwood had been educated. She visited Lyme Regis, and there is mention of the Cobb. She saw London from the top of St Paul's, and London was much smaller then than it is now. She changed from one charming house to another, and several distinguished literary gentlemen paid her compliments and came to tea. When the dining-room ceiling fell down it did not fall on her head, and when she took a ticket in a lottery she did win the prize. If in the foregoing sentences there are any words of more than two syllables, it is our fault and not Miss Hill's; and to do that writer justice, there are not many whole sentences in the book which are neither quoted from Miss Mitford nor supported by the authority of Mr Crissy.

But how dangerous a thing is life! Can one be sure that anything not wholly made of mahogany will to the very end stand empty in the sun? Even cupboards have their secret springs, and when, inadvertently we are sure, Miss Hill touches this one, out, terrible to relate, topples a stout old gentleman. In plain English, Miss Mitford had a father. There is nothing actually improper in that. Many women have had fathers. But Miss Mitford's father was kept in a cupboard; that is to say, he was not a nice father. Miss Hill even goes so far as to conjecture that when 'an imposing procession of neighbours and friends' followed him to the grave, 'we cannot help thinking that this was more to show sympathy and respect for Miss Mitford than from special respect for him'. Severe as the judgement is, the gluttonous, bibulous, amorous old man did something to deserve it. The less said about him the better. Only, if from your earliest childhood your father has gambled and speculated, first with your mother's fortune, then with your own, spent your earnings, driven you to earn more, and spent that too;

if in old age he has lain upon a sofa and insisted that fresh air is bad for daughters; if, dying at length, he has left debts that can only be paid by selling everything you have or sponging upon the charity of friends – then even a lady sometimes raises her voice. Miss Mitford herself spoke out once. 'It was grief to go; there I had toiled and striven and tasted as deeply of bitter anxiety, of fear, and of hope as often falls to the lot of woman.' What language for a lady to use! for a lady, too, who owns a teapot. There is a drawing of the teapot at the bottom of the page. But it is now of no avail; Miss Mitford has smashed it to smithereens. That is the worst of writing about ladies; they have fathers as well as teapots. On the other hand, some pieces of Dr Mitford's Wedgwood dinner service are still in existence, and a copy of Adam's Geography, which Mary won as a prize at school, is 'in our temporary possession'. If there is nothing improper in the suggestion, might not the next book be devoted entirely to them?

'Clara Butt: Her Life Story'

Miss Butt is six foot two, and her stature is faithfully reflected in her biography. Her biographer makes us feel that Miss Butt is a great deal bigger than the ordinary human being. She writes in a strain of adulation which is fitted for a giantess. And in some respects undoubtedly this is an accurate view of anyone with a voice of the calibre of Miss Butt's. Ordinary limits cease to have any meaning for them. When her voice boomed out everything went down before it. The middle-class girl – she is descended from Theodore Hook by the way – became the friend of Empresses. She mixed familiarly with Kings and Princes. She seems possessed not only of the height but of the temper of the Gods. Wherever she goes people fall down before her. All her efforts are crowned with success. Yet Miss Ponder writes well enough to give us the impression that Clara Butt is no lay figure. She is obviously a woman of gigantic vitality. She was able to hold her own with conductors and professors long before she had her fame to back her. Nothing annoys her more than the legend that she takes her work easily. Few people could have sung 'Abide with me', as she did, with a fly stuck in her throat. But while the book gives a lively and enthusiastic account of Clara Butt, it is strange how seldom music is mentioned. The Empress of Germany is much more important.

The Dream

This is a depressing book. It leaves one with a feeling not of humiliation, that is too strong a word, nor of disgust, that is too strong also. It makes us feel — it is to Mr Bullock's credit as a biographer — that we have been watching a stout white dog performing tricks in front of an audience which eggs it on, but at the same time jeers. There is nothing in the life and death of a best-seller that need cause us this queasiness. The lives of those glorious geese Florence Barclay and Ella Wheeler Wilcox can be read without a blush for them or for ourselves. They were performers too — conjurors who tumbled bank notes, billiard balls, fluttering pigeons out of very seedy hats. But they lived, and they lived with such gusto that no one can fail to share it. With Marie Corelli it was different.

Her life began with a trick and rather a shady trick. The editor of the *Illustrated London News*, a married man, 'wandering round Stratford-on-Avon church' fell in love with a woman. That bald statement must be draped. Dr Mackay committed an immoral act with a female who was not of his own social standing. 'This unwelcome flowering of his lighter moments', as Mr Bullock puts it — Corelliism is catching — was a child. But she was not called Marie and she was not called Corelli. Those were names that she invented later to drape the fact. Most of her childhood was spent draping facts in the 'Dream Hole', a mossy retreat in a dell at Box Hill. Sometimes George Meredith appeared for a moment among the tendrils. But she never saw him. Wrapped in what she called later 'the flitting phantasmagoria of the universal dream' she saw only one person – herself. And that self, sometimes called Thelma, sometimes Mavis Clare, draped in white satin, hung with pure lilies, and exhibited twice a year in stout volumes for which the public paid her ten thousand pounds apiece, is as damning an indictment of Victorian taste in one way as the Albert Memorial is in another. Of those two excrescences, perhaps that which we call Marie Corelli is the more painful. The Albert Memorial is empty; but within the other erection was a live human being. It was not her fault; society blew that golden bubble, as Miss Corelli herself might have written, from the black seed of shame. She was ashamed of her face, of her accent, of her poverty. Most girls, as empty-headed and commonplace as she was, would have shared her shame, but they would have hidden it – under the tablecloth, behind the chiffonier. But nature had endowed her with a prodigious power of making public confession of this small ignoble vice. Instead of hiding herself, she exposed herself. From her earliest days she had a rage for publicity. 'I'll be "somebody",' she told her governess. 'I'll be as unlike anybody else as I can!' 'That would hardly be wise,' said Miss Knox placidly. 'You would then be called eccentric.' But Miss Knox need not have been afraid. Marie Corelli did not wish to be unlike anybody else; she wanted to be as like everybody else in general and the British aristocracy in particular as it was possible to be. But to attain that object she had only one weapon – the dream. Dreams, apparently, if made of the right material, can be astonishingly effective. She dreamt so hard, she dreamt so efficiently, that with two exceptions all her dreams came true. Not even Marie Corelli could dream her shifty half-brother into the greatest of English poets, though she worked hard to 'get him made Poet Laureate', or transform her very dubious father into an eminent Victorian man of letters. All that she could do for Dr Mackay was to engage the Caledonian pipers to play at his funeral and to postpone that function from a foggy day to a fine one in order that his last appearance might be given full publicity. Otherwise all her dreams materialised. Ponies, motor-cars, dresses, houses furnished 'like the tea lounge at the Earl's Court Exhibition', gondolas, expensively-bound editions of Shakespeare – all were hers. Cheques accumulated. Invitations showered. The Prince of Wales held her hand in his. 'Out of small things what wonders rise,' he murmured. Gladstone called on her and stayed for two hours. '*Ardath*', he is reported to have said, 'is a magnificent conception.' On Easter Sunday the Dean of Westminster quoted *Barabbas* from the pulpit. No words, the Dean said, could be more beautiful. Rostand translated her novels. The whole audience at Stratford-on-Avon rose to its feet when she came into the theatre.

All her dreams came true. But it was the dream that killed her. For inside that ever-thickening carapace of solid dream the commonplace vigorous little woman gradually ceased to live. She became harder, duller, more prudish, more conventional; and at the same time more envious and more uneasy. The only remedy that revived her was publicity. And like other drug-takers she could only live by increasing the dose. Her tricks became more and more extravagant. On May Day she drove through the streets behind ponies wreathed in flowers; she floated down the Avon in a gondola called *The Dream* with a real gondolier in a scarlet sash. The press resounded with her lawsuits, her angry letters, her speeches. And then even the press turned nasty. They omitted to say that she had been present at the Braemar gathering. They gave full publicity to the fact that she had been caught hoarding sugar.

For her there is some excuse. But how are we to excuse the audience that applauded the exhibition? Queen Victoria and Mr Gladstone can be excepted. The taste of the highly exalted is apt to become dropsical. And there is excuse for 'the million', as Marie Corelli called them – if her books saved one working-man from suicide, or allowed a dressmaker's drudge here and there to dream that she, too, was Thelma or Mavis Clare, there were no films then to sustain them with plush and glow and rapture after the day's work. But what are we to say of Oscar Wilde? His compliments may have been ambiguous; but he paid them, and he printed her stories. And what are we to say of the great ladies of her adored aristocracy? 'She is a common little thing.' one of them remarked. But no lunch or dinner party was complete without her. And what are we to say of Mr Arthur Severn? 'Pendennis' she called him. He accepted her hospitality, tolerated that effusion which she was pleased to call her passion, and then made fun of her accent. 'Ouwels' she said instead of 'owls', and he laughed at her. And what are we to say of the press that levelled all its cameras at the stout ugly old woman who was ashamed of her face; and because she was ashamed of her birth, 'got busy' about the mother – was her name Cody, or was it Kirtland? – was she a bricklayer's daughter or an Italian countess? – who had borne this illegitimate child?

But though it would be a relief to end in a burst of righteous indignation, the worst of this book is that it provokes no such glow, but only the queasiness with which we watch a decked-up dog performing rather ordinary tricks. It is a relief when the performance is over. Only, unfortunately, that is not altogether the fact. For still at Stratford-on-Avon Mason Croft is kept precisely as it was when Marie Corelli lived there. There is the silver inkpot still full of ink as she left it; the hands of the clock still point to 7.15 as they did when she died; all her manuscripts are carefully preserved under glass cases; and 'the large, empty bed, covered with a heavy white quilt, which is more awe-inspiring than a corpse, as a scarcely clothed dancer excites more than does a nude' awaits the dreamer. So Stratford-on-Avon, along with other relics, preserves a lasting monument to the taste of the Victorian age.

The British Empire

The Royal Academy

'The motor-cars of Empire – the bodyguard of Europe – the stainless knight of Belgium' – such is our English romance that nine out of ten of those passing from the indiscriminate variety of Piccadilly to the courtyard of Burlington House do homage to the embattled tyres and the kingly presence of Albert on his high-minded charger with some nonsense of this sort. They are, of course, only the motor-cars of the rich grouped round a statue; but whether the quadrangle in which they stand radiates back the significance of everything fourfold, so that King Albert and the motor-cars exude the essence of kingliness and the soul of vehicular traffic, or whether the crowd is the cause of it, or the ceremonious steps leading up, the swing-doors admitting and the flunkeys fawning, it is true that, once you are within the precincts, everything appears symbolic, and the state of mind in which you ascend the broad stairs to the picture galleries is both heated and romantic.

Whatever visions we may have indulged, we find ourselves on entering confronted by a lady in full evening dress. She stands at the top of a staircase, one hand loosely closed round a sheaf of lilies, while the other is about to greet someone of distinction who advances towards her up the stairs. Not a hair is out of place. Her lips are just parted. She is about to say, 'How nice of you to come!' But such is the skill of the artist that one does not willingly cross the range of her cordial and yet condescending eye. One prefers to look at her obliquely. She said, 'How nice of you to come!' so often and so graciously while I stood there that at last my eye wandered off in search of people of sufficient distinction for her to say it to. There was no difficulty in finding them. Here was a nobleman in a kilt, the Duke of R.; here a young officer in khaki, and, to keep him company, the head and shoulders of a young girl, whose upturned eyes and pouting lips appear to be entreating the sky to be bluer, roses to be redder, ices to be sweeter, and men to be manlier for her sake. To do her justice, the gallant youth seemed to respond. As they stepped up the staircase to the lady in foaming white he vowed that come what might – the flag of England – sweet chimes of home – a woman's honour – an Englishman's word – only a scrap of paper – for your sake, Alice – God save the King – and all the rest of it. The range of her vocabulary was more limited. She kept her gaze upon the sky or the ice or whatever it might be with a simple sincerity which was enforced by a single row of pearls and a little drapery of white tulle about the shoulders. 'How nice of you to come!' said the hostess once more. But immediately behind them stumped the Duke, a bluff nobleman, 'more at home on the brae-side than among these kickshaws and knick-knacks, my lady. Splendid sport. Twenty antlers and Buck Royal. Clean between the eyes, eh what? Out all day. Never know when I'm done. Cold bath, hard bed, glass of whiskey. A mere nothing. Damned foreigners. Post of duty. The Guard dies, but never surrenders. The ladies of our family – Up, Guards, and at them! Gentlemen –' and, as he utters the last words in a voice choked with emotion, the entire company swing round upon their heels, displaying only a hind view of their perfectly fitting mess-jackets, since there are some sights that it is not good for a man to look upon.

The scene, though not all the phrases, comes from a story by Rudyard Kipling. But scenes from Rudyard Kipling must take place with astonishing frequency at these parties in order that the English maidens and gallant officers may have occasion to insist upon their chastity on the one hand and protect it on the other, without which, so far as one can see, there would be no reason for their existence. Therefore it was natural to look about me, a little shyly, for the sinister person of the seducer. There is, I can truthfully say, no such cur in the whole of the Royal Academy; and it was only when I had gone through the rooms twice and was about to inform the maiden that her apprehensions, though highly creditable, were in no way necessary that my eye was caught by the white underside of an excessively fine fish. 'The Duke caught that!' I exclaimed, being still within the radius of the ducal glory. But I was wrong. Though fine enough, the fish, as a second glance put it beyond a doubt, was not ducal; its triangular shape, let alone the fact that a small urchin in corduroys held it suspended by the tail, was enough to start me in the right direction. Ah, yes – the harvest of the sea, toilers of the deep, a fisherman's home, nature's bounty – such phrases formed themselves with alarming rapidity – but to descend to details. The picture, No. 306, represents a young woman holding a baby on her knee. The child is playing with the rough model of a ship; the large fish is being dangled before his eyes by a brother a year or two older in a pair of corduroys which have been cut down from those worn by the fisherman engaged in cleaning cod on the edge of the waves. Judging from the superb rosiness, fatness, and blueness of every object depicted, even the sea itself wearing the look of a prize animal tricked out for a fair, it seemed certain that the artist intended a compliment in a general way to the island race. But something in the woman's eye arrested me. A veil of white dimmed the straightforward lustre. It is thus that painters represent the tears that do not fall. But what, we asked, had this great hulk of a matron surrounded by fish, any one of which was worth eighteenpence the pound, to cry for? Look at the little boy's breeches. They are not, if you look closely, of the same pattern as the fisherman's. Once that fact is grasped, the story reels itself out like a line with a salmon on the end of it. Don't the waves break with a sound of mockery on the beach? Don't her eyes cloud with memories at the sight of a toy boat? It is not always summer. The sea has another voice than this; and, since her husband will never want his breeches any more – but the story when written out is painful, and rather obvious into the bargain.

The point of a good Academy picture is that you can search the canvas for ten minutes or so and still be doubtful whether you have extracted the whole meaning. There is, for example, No. 248, 'Cocaine'. A young man in evening dress lies, drugged, with his head upon the pink satin of a woman's knee. The ornamental clock assures us that it is exactly eleven minutes to five. The burning lamp proves that it is dawn. He, then, has come home to find her waiting? She has interrupted his debauch? For my part, I prefer to imagine what in painters' language (a tongue well worth separate study) would be called 'a dreary vigil'. There she has sat since eight-thirty, alone, in pink satin. Once she rose and pressed the photograph in the silver frame to her lips. She might have married that man (unless it is her father, of which one cannot be sure). She was a thoughtless girl, and he left her to meet his death on the field of battle.

Through her tears she gazes at the next photograph – presumably that of a baby (again the painter has been content with a suggestion). As she looks a hand fumbles at the door. 'Thank God!' she cries as her husband staggers in and falls helpless across her knees, 'thank God our Teddy died!' So there she sits, staring disillusionment in the eyes, and whether she gives way to temptation, or breathes a vow to the photographs, or gets him to bed before the maid comes down, or sits there for ever, must be left to the imagination of the onlooker.

But the queer thing is that one wants to be her. For a moment one pretends that one sits alone, disillusioned, in pink satin. And then people in the little group of gazers begin to boast that they have known sadder cases themselves. Friends of theirs took cocaine. 'I myself as a boy for a joke –' 'No, George – but how fearfully rash!' Everyone wished to cap that story with a better, save for one lady who, from her expression, was acting the part of consoler, had got the poor thing to bed, undressed her, soothed her, and even spoken with considerable sharpness to that unworthy brute, unfit to be a husband, before she moved on in a pleasant glow of self-satisfaction. Every picture before which one of these little groups had gathered seemed to radiate the strange power to make the beholder more heroic and more romantic; memories of childhood, visions of possibilities, illusions of all kinds poured down upon us from the walls. In a cooler mood one might accuse the painters of some exaggeration. There must be well over ten thousand delphiniums in the Royal Academy, and not one is other than a perfect specimen. The condition of the turf is beyond praise. The sun is exquisitely adapted to the needs of the sundials. The yew hedges are irreproachable; the manor house a miracle of timeworn dignity; and as for the old man with a scythe, the girl at the well, the village donkey, the widow lady, the gipsies' caravan, the boy with a rod, each is not only the saddest, sweetest, quaintest, most picturesque, tenderest, jolliest of its kind, but has a symbolical meaning much to the credit of England. The geese are English geese, and even the polar bears, though they have not that advantage, seem, such is the persuasion of the atmosphere, to be turning to carriage rugs as we look at them.

It is indeed a very powerful atmosphere; so charged with manliness and womanliness, pathos and purity, sunsets and Union Jacks, that the shabbiest and most suburban catch a reflection of the rosy glow. 'This is England! these are the English!' one might explain if a foreigner were at hand. But one need not say that to one's compatriots. They are, perhaps, not quite up to the level of the pictures. Some are meagre; others obese; many have put on what is too obviously the only complete outfit that they possess. But the legend on the catalogue explains any such discrepancy in a convincing manner. 'To give unto them beauty for ashes. Isaiah lxi. 3' – that is the office of this exhibition. Our ashes will be transformed if only we expose them openly enough to the benignant influence of the canvas. So we look again at the Lord Chancellor and Mr Balfour, at the Lady B., at the Duke of R., at Mr Ennever of the Pelman Institute, at officers of all descriptions, architects, surgeons, peers, dentists, doctors, lawyers, archbishops, roses, sundials, battlefields, fish, and Skye terriers. From wall to wall, glowing with colour, glistening with oil, framed in gilt, and protected by glass, they ogle and elevate, inspire and command. But they overdo it. One is not altogether such a bundle of ashes as they suppose, or sometimes the magic fails to work. A large picture by Mr Sargent called

'Gassed' at last pricked some nerve of protest, or perhaps of humanity. In order to emphasise his point that the soldiers wearing bandages round their eyes cannot see, and therefore claim our compassion, he makes one of them raise his leg to the level of his elbow in order to mount a step an inch or two above the ground. This little piece of over-emphasis was the final scratch of the surgeon's knife which is said to hurt more than the whole operation. After all, one had been jabbed and stabbed, slashed and sliced for close on two hours. The lady began it, the Duke continued it; little children had wrung tears; great men extorted veneration. From first to last each canvas had rubbed in some emotion, and what the paint failed to say the catalogue had enforced in words. But Mr Sargent was the last straw. Suddenly the great rooms rang like a parrot-house with the intolerable vociferations of gaudy and brainless birds. How they shrieked and gibbered! How they danced and sidled! Honour, patriotism, chastity, wealth, success, importance, position, patronage, power – their cries rang and echoed from all quarters. 'Anywhere, anywhere, out of this world!' was the only exclamation with which one could stave off the brazen din as one fled downstairs, out of doors, round the motor-cars, beneath the disdain of the horse and its rider, and so out into the comparative sobriety of Piccadilly. No doubt the reaction was excessive; and I must leave it to Mr Roger Fry to decide whether the emotions here recorded are the proper result of one thousand six hundred and seventy-four works of art.

Thunder at Wembley

It is nature that is the ruin of Wembley; yet it is difficult to see what steps Lord Stevenson, Lieutenant-General Sir Travers Clarke, and the Duke of Devonshire could have taken to keep her out. They might have eradicated the grass and felled the chestnut trees; even so the thrushes would have got in, and there would always have been the sky. At Earls Court and the White City, so far as memory serves, there was little trouble from this source. The area was too small; the light was too brilliant. If a single real moth strayed in to dally with the arc lamps he was at once transformed into a dizzy reveller; if a laburnum tree shook her tassels, spangles of limelight floated in the violet and crimson air. Everything was intoxicated and transformed. But at Wembley nothing is changed and nobody is drunk. They say, indeed, that there is a restaurant where each diner is forced to spend a guinea upon his dinner. What vistas of cold ham that statement calls forth! What pyramids of rolls! What gallons of tea and coffee! For it is unthinkable that there should be champagne, plovers' eggs, or peaches at Wembley. And for six and eightpence two people can buy as much ham and bread as they need. Six and eightpence is not a large sum; but neither is it a small sum. It is a moderate sum, a mediocre sum. It is the prevailing sum at Wembley. You look through an open door at a regiment of motor-cars aligned in avenues.

They are not opulent and powerful; they are not flimsy and cheap. Six and eightpence seems to be the price of each of them. It is the same with the machines for crushing gravel. One can imagine better; one can imagine worse. The machine before us is a serviceable type, and costs, inevitably, six and eightpence. Dress fabrics, rope, table linen, old masters, sugar, wheat, filigree silver, pepper, birds' nests (edible, and exported to Hong-Kong), camphor, bees-wax, rattans, and the rest – why trouble to ask the price? One knows beforehand – six and eightpence. As for the buildings themselves, those vast, smooth, grey palaces, no vulgar riot of ideas tumbled expensively in their architect's head; equally, cheapness was abhorrent to him, and vulgarity anathema. Per perch, rod, or square foot, however ferro-concrete palaces are sold, they too work out at six and eightpence.

But then, just as one is beginning a little wearily to fumble with those two fine words – democracy, mediocrity – nature asserts herself where one would least look to find her – in clergymen, school children, girls, young men, invalids in bath-chairs. They pass, quietly, silently, in coveys, in groups, sometimes alone. They mount the enormous staircases; they stand in queues to have their spectacles rectified gratis; to have their fountainpens filled gratis; they gaze respectfully into sacks of grain; glance reverently at mowing machines from Canada; now and again stoop to remove some paper bag or banana skin and place it in the receptacles provided for that purpose at frequent intervals along the avenues. But what has happened to our contemporaries? Each is beautiful; each is stately. Can it be that one is seeing human beings for the first time? In streets they hurry; in houses they talk; they are bankers in banks; sell shoes in shops. Here against the enormous background of ferro-concrete Britain, of rosy Burma, at large, unoccupied, they reveal themselves simply as human beings, creatures of leisure, civilisation, and dignity; a little languid perhaps, a little attenuated, but a product to be proud of. Indeed, they are the ruin of the Exhibition. The Duke of Devonshire and his colleagues should have kept them out. As you watch them trailing and flowing, dreaming and speculating, admiring this coffee-grinder, that milk and cream separator, the rest of the show becomes insignificant. And what, one asks, is the spell it lays upon them? How, with all this dignity of their own, can they bring themselves to believe in that?

But this cynical reflection, at once so chill and so superior, was made, of course, by the thrush. Down in the Amusement Compound, by some grave oversight on the part of the Committee, several trees and rhododendron bushes have been allowed to remain; and these, as anybody could have foretold, attract the birds. As you wait your turn to be hoisted into mid-air, it is impossible not to hear the thrush singing. You look up, and discover a whole chestnut tree with its blossoms standing; you look down, and see ordinary grass scattered with petals, harbouring insects, sprinkled with stray wild flowers. The gramophone does its best; they light a horse-shoe of fairy lamps above the Jack and Jill; a man bangs a bladder and implores you to come and tickle monkeys; boatloads of serious men are poised on the heights of the scenic railway; but all is vain. The cry of ecstasy that should have split the sky as the boat dropped to its doom patters from leaf to leaf, dies, falls flat, while the thrush proceeds with his statement. And then some woman, in the row of red-brick villas outside the grounds, comes out and wrings a dish-cloth in the backyard. All this the Duke of Devonshire should have prevented.

The problem of the sky, however, remains. Is it, one

wonders, lying back limp but acquiescent in a green deckchair, part of the Exhibition? Is it lending itself with exquisite tact to show off to the best advantage snowy Palestine, ruddy Burma, sand-coloured Canada, and the minarets and pagodas of our possessions in the East? So quietly it suffers all these domes and palaces to melt into its breast; receives them with such sombre and tender discretion; so exquisitely allows the rear lamp of Jack and Jill and the Monkey-Teasers to bear themselves like stars. But even as we watch and admire what we would fain credit to the forethought of Lieutenant-General Sir Travers Clarke, a rushing sound is heard. Is it the wind, or is it the British Empire Exhibition? It is both. The wind is rising and shuffling along the avenues; the Massed Bands of Empire are assembling and marching to the Stadium. Men like pin-cushions, men like pouter pigeons, men like pillar-boxes, pass in procession. Dust swirls after them. Admirably impassive, the Bands of Empire march on. Soon they will have entered the fortress; soon the gates will have clanged. But let them hasten! For either the sky has misread her directions, or some appalling catastrophe is impending. The sky is livid, lurid, sulphurine. It is in violent commotion. It is whirling water-spouts of cloud into the air; of dust in the Exhibition. Dust swirls down the avenues, hisses and hurries like erected cobras round the corners. Pagodas are dissolving in dust. Ferro-concrete is fallible. Colonies are perishing and dispersing in spray of inconceivable beauty and terror which some malignant power illuminates. Ash and violet are the colours of its decay. From every quarter human beings come flying – clergymen, school children, invalids in bath-chairs. They fly with outstretched arms, and a vast sound of wailing rolls before them, but there is neither confusion nor dismay. Humanity is rushing to destruction, but humanity is accepting its doom. Canada opens a frail tent of shelter. Clergymen and school children gain its portals. Out in the open, under a cloud of electric silver, the Bands of Empire strike up. The bagpipes neigh. Clergy, school children, and invalids group themselves round the Prince of Wales in butter. Cracks like the white roots of trees spread themselves across the firmament. The Empire is perishing; the bands are playing; the Exhibition is in ruins. For that is what comes of letting in the sky.

Class

Middlebrow

To the Editor of the *New Statesman*

Sir,

Will you allow me to draw your attention to the fact that in a review of a book by me (October   ) your reviewer omitted to use the word Highbrow? The review, save for that omission, gave me so much pleasure that I am driven to ask you, at the risk of appearing unduly egotistical, whether your reviewer, a man of obvious intelligence, intended to deny my claim to that title? I say 'claim', for surely I may claim that title when a great critic, who is also a great novelist, a rare and enviable combination, always calls me a highbrow when he condescends to notice my work in a great newspaper; and, further, always finds space to inform not only myself, who know it already, but the whole British Empire, who hang on his words, that I live in Bloomsbury? Is your critic unaware of that fact too? Or does he, for all his intelligence, maintain that it is unnecessary in reviewing a book to add the postal address of the writer?

His answer to these questions, though of real value to me, is of no possible interest to the public at large. Of that I am well aware. But since larger issues are involved, since the Battle of the Brows troubles, I am told, the evening air, since the finest minds of our age have lately been engaged in debating, not without that passion which befits a noble cause, what a highbrow is and what a lowbrow, which is better and which is worse, may I take this opportunity to express my opinion and at the same time draw attention to certain aspects of the question which seem to me to have been unfortunately overlooked?

Now there can be no two opinions as to what a highbrow is. He is the man or woman of thoroughbred intelligence who rides his mind at a gallop across country in pursuit of an idea. That is why I have always been so proud to be called highbrow. That is why, if I could be more of a highbrow I would. I honour and respect highbrows. Some of my relations have been highbrows; and some, but by no means all, of my friends. To be a highbrow, a complete and representative highbrow, a highbrow like Shakespeare, Dickens, Byron, Shelley, Keats, Charlotte Brontë, Scott, Jane Austen, Flaubert, Hardy or Henry James – to name a few highbrows from the same profession chosen at random – is of course beyond the wildest dreams of my imagination. And, though I would cheerfully lay myself down in the dust and kiss the print of their feet, no person of sense will deny that this passionate preoccupation of theirs – riding across country in pursuit of ideas – often leads to disaster. Undoubtedly, they come fearful croppers. Take Shelley – what a mess he made of his life! And Byron, getting into bed with first one woman and then another and dying in the mud at Missolonghi. Look at Keats, loving poetry and Fanny Brawne so intemperately that he pined and died of consumption at the age of twenty-six. Charlotte Brontë again – I have been assured on good authority that Charlotte Brontë was, with the possible exception of Emily, the worst governess in the British Isles. Then there was Scott – he went bankrupt, and left, together with a few magnificent novels, one house, Abbotsford, which is perhaps the ugliest in the whole Empire. But surely these instances are enough – I need not further labour the point that highbrows, for some reason or another, are wholly incapable of dealing successfully with what is called real life. That is why, and here I come to a point that is often surprisingly ignored, they honour so wholeheartedly and depend so completely upon those who are called lowbrows. By a lowbrow is meant of course a man or a woman of thoroughbred vitality who rides his body in pursuit of a living at a gallop across life. That is why I honour and respect lowbrows – and I have never known a highbrow who did not. In so far as I am a highbrow (and my imperfections in that line are well known to me) I love lowbrows; I study them; I always sit next the conductor in an omnibus and try to get him to tell me what it is like – being a conductor. In whatever company I am I always try to know what it is like – being a conductor, being a woman with ten children and thirty-five shillings a week, being a stockbroker, being an admiral, being a bank clerk, being a dressmaker, being a duchess, being a miner, being a cook, being a prostitute. All that lowbrows do is of surpassing interest and wonder to me, because, in so far as I am a highbrow, I cannot do things myself.

This brings me to another point which is also surprisingly overlooked. Lowbrows need highbrows and honour them just as much as highbrows need lowbrows and honour them. This too is not a matter that requires much demon-stration. You have only to stroll along the Strand on a wet winter's night and watch the crowds lining up to get into the movies. These lowbrows are waiting, after the day's work, in the rain, sometimes for hours, to get into the cheap seats and sit in hot theatres in order to see what their lives look like. Since they are lowbrows, engaged magnificently and adventurously in riding full tilt from one end of life to the other in pursuit of a living, they cannot see themselves doing it. Yet nothing interests them more. Nothing matters to them more. It is one of the prime necessities of life to them – to be shown what life looks like. And the highbrows, of course, are the only people who can show them. Since they are the only people who do not do things, they are the only people who can see things being done. This is so – and so it is I am certain; nevertheless we are told – the air buzzes with it by night, the Press booms with it by day, the very donkeys in the fields do nothing but bray it, the very curs in the streets do nothing but bark it – 'Highbrows hate lowbrows! Lowbrows hate highbrows!' – when highbrows need lowbrows, when lowbrows need highbrows, when they cannot exist apart, when one is the complement and other side of the other! How has such a lie come into existence? Who has set this malicious gossip afloat?

There can be no doubt about that either. It is the doing of the middlebrows. They are the people, I confess, that I seldom regard with entire cordiality. They are the go-betweens; they are the busybodies who run from one to the other with their tittle tattle and make all the mischief – the middlebrows, I repeat. But what, you may ask, is a middlebrow? And that, to tell the truth, is no easy question to answer. They are neither one thing nor the other. They are not highbrows, whose brows are high; nor lowbrows, whose brows are low. Their brows are betwixt and between. They do not live in Bloomsbury which is on high ground; nor in Chelsea, which is on low ground. Since they must live somewhere presumably, they live perhaps in South Kensington, which is betwixt and between. The middlebrow is the man, or woman, of middlebred intelligence who ambles and saunters now on this side of the hedge, now on that, in pursuit of no single object, neither art itself nor life itself, but both mixed indistinguishably, and rather nastily, with money, fame, power, or prestige. The middlebrow curries favour with both sides equally. He goes to the lowbrows and tells them that while he is not quite one of them, he is almost their friend. Next moment he rings up the highbrows and asks them with equal geniality whether he may not come to tea. Now there are highbrows – I myself have known duchesses who were highbrows, also charwomen, and they have both told me with that vigour of language which so often unites the aristocracy with the working classes, that they would rather sit in the coal cellar, together, than in the drawing-room with middlebrows and pour out tea. I have myself been asked – but may I, for the sake of brevity, cast this scene which is only partly fictitious, into the form of fiction? – I myself, then, have been asked to come and 'see' them – how strange a passion theirs is for being 'seen'! They ring me up, therefore, at about eleven in the morning, and ask me to come to tea. I go to my wardrobe and consider, rather lugubriously, what is the right thing to wear? We highbrows may be smart, or we may be shabby; but we never have the right thing to wear. I proceed to ask next: What is the right thing to say? Which is the right knife to use? What is the right book to praise? All these are things I do not know for myself. We highbrows read what we like and do what we like and praise what we like. We also know what we dislike – for example, thin bread and butter tea. The difficulty of eating thin bread and butter in white kid gloves has always seemed to me one of life's more insuperable problems. Then I dislike bound volumes of the classics behind plate glass. Then I distrust people who call both Shakespeare and Wordsworth equally 'Bill' – it is a habit moreover that leads to confusion. And in the matter of clothes, I like people either to dress very well; or to dress very badly; I dislike the correct thing in clothes. Then there is the question of games. Being a highbrow I do not play them. But I love watching people play who have a passion for games. These middlebrows pat balls about; they poke their bats and muff their catches at cricket. And when poor Middlebrow mounts on horseback and that animal breaks into a canter, to me there is no sadder sight in all Rotten Row. To put it in a nutshell (in order to get on with the story) that tea party was not wholly a success, nor altogether a failure; for Middlebrow, who writes, following me to the door, clapped me briskly on the back, and said 'I'm sending you my book!' (Or did he call it 'stuff'?) And his book comes – sure enough, though called, so symbolically, *Keepaway*, it comes. And I read a page here, and I read a page there (I am breakfasting, as usual, in bed). And it is not well written; nor is it badly written. It is not proper, nor is it improper – in short it is betwixt and between. Now if there is any sort of book for which I have, perhaps, an imperfect sympathy, it is the betwixt and between. And so, though I suffer from the gout of a morning – but if one's ancestors for two or three centuries have tumbled into bed dead drunk one has deserved a touch of that malady – I rise. I dress. I proceed weakly to the window. I take that book in my swollen right hand and toss it gently over the hedge into the field. The hungry sheep – did I remember to say that this part of the story takes place in the country? – the hungry sheep look up but are not fed.

But to have done with fiction and its tendency to lapse into poetry – I will now report a perfectly prosaic

conversation in words of one syllable. I often ask my friends
the lowbrows, over our muffins and honey, why it is that
while we, the highbrows, never buy a middlebrow book,
or go to a middlebrow lecture, or read, unless we are paid
for doing so, a middlebrow review, they, on the contrary,
take these middlebrow activities so seriously? Why, I ask
(not of course on the wireless), are you so damnably modest?
Do you think that a description of your lives, as they are,
is too sordid and too mean to be beautiful? Is that why
you prefer the middlebrow version of what they have the
impudence to call real humanity? – this mixture of geniality
and sentiment stuck together with a sticky slime of calf's-foot
jelly? The truth, if you would only believe it, is much more
beautiful than any lie. Then again, I continue, how can
you let the middlebrows teach *you* how to write? – you,
who write so beautifully when you write naturally, that I
would give both my hands to write as you do – for which
reason I never attempt it, but do my best to learn the art
of writing as a highbrow should. And again, I press on,
brandishing a muffin on the point of a tea spoon, how dare
the middlebrows teach *you* how to read – Shakespeare for
instance? All you have to do is to read him. The Cambridge
edition is both good and cheap. If you find *Hamlet* difficult,
ask him to tea. He is a highbrow. Ask Ophelia to meet
him. She is a lowbrow. Talk to them, as you talk to me,
and you will know more about Shakespeare than all the
middlebrows in the world can teach you – I do not think,
by the way, from certain phrases that Shakespeare liked
middlebrows, or Pope either.

To all this the lowbrows reply – but I cannot imitate
their style of talking – that they consider themselves to be
common people without education. It is very kind of the
middlebrows to try to teach them culture. And after all,

the lowbrows continue, middlebrows, like other people, have to make money. There must be money in teaching and in writing books about Shakespeare. We all have to earn our livings nowadays, my friends the lowbrows remind me. I quite agree. Even those of us whose Aunts came a cropper riding in India and left them an annual income of four hundred and fifty pounds, now reduced, thanks to the war and other luxuries, to little more than two hundred odd, even we have to do that. And we do it, too, by writing about anybody who seems amusing – enough has been written about Shakespeare – Shakespeare hardly pays. We highbrows, I agree, have to earn our livings; but when we have earned enough to live on, then we live. When the middlebrows, on the contrary, have earned enough to live on, they go on earning enough to buy – what are the things that middlebrows always buy? Queen Anne furniture (faked, but none the less expensive); first editions of dead writers – always the worst; pictures, or reproductions from pictures, by dead painters; houses in what is called 'the Georgian style' – but never anything new, never a picture by a living painter, or a chair by a living carpenter, or books by living writers, for to buy living art requires living taste. And, as that kind of art and that kind of taste are what middlebrows call 'highbrow', 'Bloomsbury', poor middle-brow spends vast sums on sham antiques, and has to keep at it scribbling away, year in, year out, while we highbrows ring each other up, and are off for a day's jaunt into the country. That is the worst of course of living in a set – one likes being with one's friends.

Have I then made my point clear, sir, that the true battle in my opinion lies not between highbrow and lowbrow, but between highbrows and lowbrows joined together in blood brotherhood against the bloodless and pernicious pest who comes between? If the B.B.C. stood for anything but the Betwixt and Between Company they would use their control of the air not to stir strife between brothers, but to broadcast the fact that highbrows and lowbrows must band together to exterminate a pest which is the bane of all thinking and living. It may be, to quote from your advertisement columns, that 'terrifically sensitive' lady novelists overestimate the dampness and dinginess of this fungoid growth. But all I can say is that when, lapsing into that stream which people call, so oddly, consciousness, and gathering wool from the sheep that have been mentioned above, I ramble round my garden in the suburbs, middlebrow seems to me to be everywhere. 'What's that?' I cry. 'Middlebrow on the cabbages? Middlebrow infecting that poor old sheep? And what about the moon?' I look up and, behold, the moon is under eclipse. 'Middlebrow at it again!' I exclaim. 'Middlebrow obscuring, dulling, tarnishing and coarsening even the silver edge of Heaven's own scythe.' (I 'draw near to poetry,' see advt.) And then my thoughts, as Freud assures us thoughts will do, rush (Middlebrow's saunter and simper, out of respect for the Censor) to sex, and I ask of the sea-gulls who are crying on desolate sea sands and of the farm hands who are coming home rather drunk to their wives, what will become of us, men and women, if Middlebrow has his way with us, and there is only a middle sex but no husbands or wives? The next remark I address with the utmost humility to the Prime Minister. 'What, sir,' I demand, 'will be the fate of the British Empire and of our Dominions Across the Seas if Middlebrows prevail? Will you not, sir, read a pronouncement of an authoritative nature from Broadcasting House?'

Such are the thoughts, such are the fancies that visit 'cultured invalidish ladies with private means' (see advt.)

when they stroll in their suburban gardens and look at the cabbages and at the red brick villas that have been built by middlebrows so that middlebrows may look at the view. Such are the thoughts 'at once gay and tragic and deeply feminine' (see advt.) of one who has not yet 'been driven out of Bloomsbury' (advt. again), a place where lowbrows and highbrows live happily together on equal terms and priests are not, nor priestesses, and, to be quite frank, the adjective 'priestly' is neither often heard nor held in high esteem. Such are the thoughts of one who will stay in Bloomsbury until the Duke of Bedford, rightly concerned for the respectability of his squares, raises the rent so high that Bloomsbury is safe for middlebrows to live in. Then she will leave.

May I conclude, as I began, by thanking your reviewer for his very courteous and interesting review, but may I tell him that though he did not, for reasons best known to himself, call me a highbrow, there is no name in the world that I prefer? I ask nothing better than that all reviewers, for ever, and everywhere, should call me a highbrow. I will do my best to oblige them. If they like to add Bloomsbury, W.C.1, that is the correct postal address, and my telephone number is in the Directory. But if your reviewer, or any other reviewer, dares hint that I live in South Kensington, I will sue him for libel. If any human being, man, woman, dog, cat or half-crushed worm dares call me 'middlebrow' I will take my pen and stab him, dead.

Yours etc., Virginia Woolf.

Introductory Letter to Margaret Llewelyn Davies

When you asked me to write a preface to a book which you had collected of papers by working women I replied that I would be drowned rather than write a preface to any book whatsoever. Books should stand on their own feet, my argument was (and I think it is a sound one). If they need shoring up by a preface here, an introduction there, they have no more right to exist than a table that needs a wad of paper under one leg in order to stand steady. But you left me the papers, and, turning them over, I saw that on this occasion the argument did not apply; this book is not a book. Turning the pages, I began to ask myself what is this book then, if it is not a book? What quality has it? What ideas does it suggest? What old arguments and memories does it rouse in me? And as all this had nothing to do with an introduction or a preface, but brought you to mind and certain pictures from the past, I stretched my hand for a sheet of notepaper and wrote the following letter addressed not to the public but to you.

You have forgotten (I wrote) a hot June morning in Newcastle in the year 1913, or at least you will not remember what I remember, because you were otherwise engaged. Your attention was entirely absorbed by a green table, several sheets of paper, and a bell. Moreover you were frequently interrupted. There was a woman wearing something like a Lord Mayor's chain round her shoulders; she took her seat perhaps at your right; there were other women without ornament save fountain pens and despatch boxes – they sat perhaps at your left. Soon a row had been formed up there on the platform, with tables and inkstands and tumblers of water; while we, many hundreds of us, scraped and shuffled and filled the entire body of some vast municipal building beneath. The proceedings somehow opened. Perhaps an organ played. Perhaps songs were sung. Then the talking and the laughing suddenly subsided. A bell struck; a figure rose; a woman took her way from among us; she mounted a platform; she spoke for precisely five minutes; she descended. Directly she sat down another woman rose; mounted the platform; spoke for precisely five minutes and descended; then a third rose, then a fourth – and so it went on, speaker following speaker, one from the right, one from the left, one from the middle, one from the background – each took her way to the stand, said what she had to say, and gave place to her successor. There was something military in the regularity of the proceeding. They were like marksmen, I thought, standing up in turn with rifle raised to aim at a target. Sometimes they missed, and there was a roar of laughter; sometimes they hit, and there was a roar of applause. But whether the particular shot hit or missed there was no doubt about the carefulness of the aim. There was no beating the bush; there were no phrases of easy eloquence. The speaker made her way to the stand primed with her subject. Determination and resolution were stamped on her face. There was so much to be said between the strokes of the bell that she could not waste one second. The moment had come for which she had been waiting, perhaps for many months. The moment had come for which she had stored hat, shoes and dress – there was an air of discreet novelty about her clothing. But above all the moment had come when she was going to speak her mind, the mind of her constituency, the mind of the women who had sent her from Devonshire, perhaps, or Sussex, or some black mining village in Yorkshire to speak their mind for them in Newcastle.

It soon became obvious that the mind which lay spread over so wide a stretch of England was a vigorous mind working with great activity. It was thinking in June 1913 of the reform of the Divorce Laws; of the taxation of land values; of the Minimum Wage. It was concerned with the care of maternity; with the Trades Board Act; with the education of children over fourteen; it was unanimously of opinion that Adult Suffrage should become a Government measure – it was thinking in short about every sort of public question, and it was thinking constructively and pugnaciously. Accrington did not see eye to eye with Halifax, nor Middlesbrough with Plymouth. There was argument and opposition; resolutions were lost and amendments won. Hands shot up stiff as swords, or were pressed as stiffly to the side. Speaker followed speaker; the morning was cut up into precise lengths of five minutes by the bell.

Meanwhile – let me try after seventeen years to sum up the thoughts that passed through the minds of your guests, who had come from London and elsewhere, not to take part, but to listen – meanwhile what was it all about? What was the meaning of it? These women were demanding divorce, education, the vote – all good things. They were demanding higher wages and shorter hours – what could be more reasonable? And yet, though it was all so reasonable, much of it so forcible, some of it so humorous, a weight of discomfort was settling and shifting itself uneasily from side to side in your visitors' minds. All these questions – perhaps this was at the bottom of it – which matter so intensely to the people here, questions of sanitation and education and wages, this demand for an extra shilling, for another year at school, for eight hours instead of nine behind a counter or in a mill, leave me, in my own blood and bones, untouched. If every reform they demand was granted this very instant it would not touch one hair of my comfortable capitalistic head. Hence my interest is merely altruistic. It is thin spread and moon coloured. There is no life blood or urgency about it. However hard I clap my hands or stamp my feet there is a hollowness in the sound which betrays me. I am a benevolent spectator. I am irretrievably cut off from the actors. I sit here hypocritically clapping and stamping, an outcast from the flock. On top of this too, my reason (it was in 1913, remember) could not help assuring me that even if the resolution, whatever it was, were carried unanimously the stamping and the clapping was an empty noise. It would pass out of the open window and become part of the clamour of the lorries and the striving of the hooves on the cobbles of Newcastle beneath – an inarticulate uproar. The mind might be active; the mind might be aggressive; but the mind was without a body; it had no legs or arms with which to enforce its will. In all that audience, among all those women who worked, who bore children, who scrubbed and cooked and bargained, there was not a single woman with a vote. Let them fire off their rifles if they liked, but they would hit no target; there were only blank cartridges inside. The thought was irritating and depressing in the extreme.

The clock had now struck half-past eleven. Thus there were still then many hours to come. And if one had reached this stage of irritation and depression by half-past eleven in the morning, into what depths of boredom and despair would one not be plunged by half-past five in the evening? How could one sit out another day of speechifying? How could one, above all, face you, our hostess, with the information that your Congress had proved so insupportably exacerbating that one was going back to London by the very first train? The only chance lay in some happy conjuring trick, some change of attitude by which the mist and blankness of the speeches could be turned to blood and bone. Otherwise they remained intolerable. But suppose one played a childish game; suppose one said, as a child says, 'Let's pretend.' 'Let's pretend,' one said to oneself, looking at the speaker, 'that I am Mrs Giles of Durham City.' A woman of that name had just turned to address us. 'I am the wife of a miner. He comes back thick with grime. First he must have his bath. Then he must have his supper. But there is only a copper. My range is crowded with saucepans. There is no getting on with the work. All my crocks are covered with dust again. Why in the Lord's name have I not hot water and electric light laid on when middle-class women . . .' So up I jump and demand passionately 'labour saving appliances and housing reform.' Up I jump in the person of Mrs Giles of Durham; in the person of Mrs Phillips of Bacup; in the person of Mrs Edwards of Wolverton. But after all the imagination is largely the child of the flesh. One could not be Mrs Giles of Durham because one's body had never stood at the wash-tub; one's hands had never wrung and scrubbed and chopped up whatever the meat may be that makes a miner's supper. The picture therefore was always letting in irrelevancies. One sat in an armchair or read a book. One saw landscapes and seascapes, perhaps Greece or Italy, where Mrs Giles or Mrs Edwards must have seen slag heaps and rows upon rows of slate-roofed houses. Something was always creeping in from a world that was not their world and making the picture false and the game too much of a game to be worth playing.

It was true that one could always correct these fancy portraits by taking a look at the actual person – at Mrs Thomas, or Mrs Langrish, or Miss Bolt of Hebden Bridge. They were worth looking at. Certainly, there were no armchairs, or electric light, or hot water laid on in their lives; no Greek hills or Mediterranean bays in their dreams. Bakers and butchers did not call for orders. They did not sign a cheque to pay the weekly bills, or order, over the telephone, a cheap but quite adequate seat at the Opera. If they travelled it was on excursion day, with food in string bags and babies in their arms. They did not stroll through the house and say, that cover must go to the wash, or those sheets need changing. They plunged their arms in hot water and scrubbed the clothes themselves. In consequence their bodies were thick-set and muscular, their hands were large, and they had the slow emphatic gestures of people who are often stiff and fall tired in a heap on hard-backed chairs. They touched nothing lightly. They gripped papers and pencils as if they were brooms. Their faces were firm and heavily folded and lined with deep lines. It seemed as if their muscles were always taut and on the stretch. Their eyes looked as if they were always set on something actual – on saucepans that were boiling over, on children who were getting into mischief. Their lips never expressed the lighter and more detached emotions that come into play when the mind is perfectly at ease about the present. No, they were not in the least detached and easy and cosmo-politan. They were indigenous and rooted to one spot. Their very names were like the stones of the field – common, grey, worn, obscure, docked of all splendours of association and romance. Of course they wanted baths and ovens and education and seventeen shillings instead of sixteen, and freedom and air and . . . 'And,' said Mrs Winthrop of Spennymoor, breaking into these thoughts with words that sounded like a refrain, 'we can wait.' . . . 'Yes,' she repeated, as if she had waited so long that the last lap of that immense vigil meant nothing for the end was in sight, 'we can wait.' And she got down rather stiffly from her perch and made her way back to her seat, an elderly woman dressed in her best clothes.

Then Mrs Potter spoke. Then Mrs Elphick. Then Mrs Holmes of Edgbaston. So it went on, and at last after innumerable speeches, after many communal meals at long tables and many arguments – the world was to be reformed, from top to bottom, in a variety of ways – after seeing Co-operative jams bottled and Co-operative biscuits made, after some song singing and ceremonies with banners, the new President received the chain of office with a kiss from the old President; the Congress dispersed; and the separate members who had stood up so valiantly and spoken out so boldly while the clock ticked its five minutes went back to Yorkshire and Wales and Sussex and Devonshire, and hung their clothes in the wardrobe and plunged their hands in the wash-tub again.

Later that summer the thoughts here so inadequately described, were again discussed, but not in a public hall hung with banners and loud with voices. The head office of the Guild, the centre from which speakers, papers, inkstands and tumblers, as I suppose, issued, was then in Hampstead. There, if I may remind you again of what you may well have forgotten, you invited us to come; you asked us to tell you how the Congress had impressed us. But I must pause on the threshold of that very dignified old house, with its eighteenth-century carvings and panelling, as we paused then in truth, for one could not enter and go upstairs without encountering Miss Kidd. Miss Kidd sat at her typewriter in the outer office. Miss Kidd, one felt, had set herself as a kind of watch-dog to ward off the meddlesome middle-class wasters of time who come prying into other people's business. Whether it was for this reason that she was dressed in a peculiar shade of deep purple I do not know. The colour seemed somehow symbolical. She was very short, but, owing to the weight which sat on her brow and the gloom which seemed to issue from her dress, she was also very heavy. An extra share of the world's grievances seemed to press upon her shoulders. When she clicked her typewriter one felt that she was making that instrument transmit messages of foreboding and ill-omen to an unheeding universe. But she relented, and like all relentings after gloom hers came with a sudden charm. Then we went upstairs, and upstairs we came upon a very different figure – upon Miss Lilian Harris, indeed, who, whether it was due to her dress which was coffee coloured, or to her smile which was serene, or to the ash-tray in which many cigarettes had come amiably to an end, seemed the image of detachment and equanimity. Had one not known that Miss Harris was to the Congress what the heart is to the remoter veins – that the great engine at Newcastle would not have thumped and throbbed without her – that she had collected and sorted and summoned and arranged that very intricate but orderly assembly of women – she would never have enlightened one. She had nothing whatever to do; she licked a few stamps and addressed a few envelopes – it was a fad of hers – that was what her manner conveyed. It was Miss Harris who moved the papers off the chairs and got the tea-cups out of the cupboard. It was she who answered questions about figures and put her hand on the right file of letters infallibly and sat listening, without saying very much, but with calm comprehension, to whatever was said.

Again let me telescope into a few sentences, and into one scene many random discussions on various occasions at various places. We said then – for you now emerged from an inner room, and if Miss Kidd was purple and Miss Harris was coffee coloured, you, speaking pictorially (and I dare not speak more explicitly) were kingfisher blue and as arrowy and decisive as that quick bird – we said then that the Congress had roused thoughts and ideas of the most diverse nature. It had been a revelation and a disillusionment. We had been humiliated and enraged. To begin with, all their talk, we said, or the greater part of it, was of matters of fact. They want baths and money. To expect us, whose minds, such as they are, fly free at the end of a short length of capital to tie ourselves down again to that narrow plot of acquisitiveness and desire is impossible. We have baths and we have money. Therefore, however much we had sympathised our sympathy was largely fictitious. It was aesthetic sympathy, the sympathy of the eye and of the imagination, not of the heart and of the nerves; and such sympathy is always physically uncomfortable. Let us explain what we mean, we said. The Guild's women are magnificent to look at. Ladies in evening dress are lovelier far, but they lack the sculpturesque quality that these working women have. And though the range of expression is narrower in working women, their few expressions have a force and an emphasis, of tragedy or humour, which the faces of ladies lack. But, at the same time, it is much better to be a lady; ladies desire Mozart and Einstein – that is, they desire things that are ends, not things that are means. Therefore to deride ladies and to imitate, as some of the speakers did, their mincing speech and little knowledge of what it pleases them to call 'reality' is, so it seems to us, not merely foolish but gives away the whole purpose of the Congress, for if it is better to be working women by all means let them remain so and not undergo the contamination which wealth and comfort bring. In spite of this, we went on, apart from prejudices and bandying compliments, undoubtedly the women at the Congress possess something which ladies lack, and something which is desirable, which is stimulating, and yet very difficult to define. One does not want to slip easily into fine phrases about 'contact with life,' about 'facing facts' and 'the teaching of experience,' for they invariably alienate the hearer, and moreover, no working man or woman works harder or is in closer touch with reality than a painter with his brush or a writer with his pen. But the quality that they have, judging from a phrase caught here and there, from a laugh, or a gesture seen in passing, is precisely the quality that Shakespeare would have enjoyed. One can fancy him slipping away from the brilliant salons of educated people to crack a joke in Mrs Robson's back kitchen. Indeed, we said, one of our most curious impressions at your Congress was that the 'poor', 'the working classes', or by whatever name you choose to call them, are not downtrodden, envious and exhausted; they are humorous and vigorous and thoroughly independent. Thus if it were possible to meet them not as masters or mistresses or customers with a counter between us, but over the wash-tub or in the parlour casually and congenially as fellow-beings with the same wishes and ends in view, a great liberation would follow, and perhaps friendship and sympathy would supervene. How many words must lurk in those women's vocabularies that have faded from ours! How many scenes must lie dormant in their eye which are unseen by ours! What images and saws and proverbial sayings must still be current with them that have never reached the surface of print, and very likely they still keep the power which we have lost of making new ones. There were many shrewd sayings in the speeches at Congress which even the weight of a public meeting could not flatten out entirely. But, we said, and here perhaps fiddled with a paper knife, or poked the fire impatiently by way of expressing our discontent, what is the use of it all? Our sympathy is fictitious, not real. Because the baker calls and we pay our bills with cheques, and our clothes are washed for us and we do not know the liver from the lights we are condemned to remain forever shut up in the confines of the middle classes, wearing tail coats and silk stockings, and called Sir or Madam as the case may be, when we are all, in truth, simply Johns and Susans. And they remain equally deprived. For we have as much to give them as they to give us – wit and detachment, learning and poetry, and all those good gifts which those who have never answered bells or minded machines enjoy by right. But the barrier is impassable. And nothing perhaps exacerbated us more at the Congress (you must have noticed at times a certain irritability) than the thought that this force of theirs, this smouldering heat which broke the crust now and then and licked the surface with a hot and fearless flame, is about to break through and melt us together so that life will be richer and books more complex and society will pool its possessions instead of segregating them – all this is going to happen inevitably, thanks to you, very largely, and to Miss Harris and to Miss Kidd – but only when we are dead.

It was thus that we tried in the Guild Office that afternoon to explain the nature of fictitious sympathy and how it differs from real sympathy and how defective it is because it is not based upon sharing the same important emotions unconsciously. It was thus that we tried to describe the contradictory and complex feelings which beset the middle-class visitor when forced to sit out a Congress of working women in silence.

Perhaps it was at this point that you unlocked a drawer and took out a packet of papers. You did not at once untie the string that fastened them. Sometimes, you said, you got a letter which you could not bring yourself to burn; once or twice a Guildswoman had at your suggestion written a few pages about her life. It might be that we should find these papers interesting; that if we read them the women would cease to be symbols and would become instead individuals. But they were very fragmentary and ungrammatical; they had been jotted down in the intervals of housework. Indeed you could not at once bring yourself to give them up, as if to expose them to other eyes were a breach of confidence. It might be that their crudity would only perplex, that the writing of people who do not know how to write – but at this point we burst in. In the first place, every Englishwoman knows how to write; in the second, even if she does not she has only to take her own life for subject and write the truth about that and not fiction or poetry for our interest to be so keenly roused that – that in short we cannot wait but must read the packet at once.

Thus pressed you did by degrees and with many delays – there was the war for example, and Miss Kidd died, and you and Lilian Harris retired from the Guild, and a testimonial was given you in a casket, and many thousands of working women tried to say how you had changed their lives – tried to say what they will feel for you to their dying day – after all these interruptions you did at last gather the papers together and finally put them in my hands early this May. There they were, typed and docketed with a few snapshots and rather faded photographs stuck between the pages. And when at last I began to read, there started up in my mind's eye the figures that I had seen all those years ago at Newcastle with such bewilderment and curiosity. But they were no longer addressing a large meeting in Newcastle from a platform, dressed in their best clothes. The hot June day with its banners and its ceremonies had vanished, and instead one looked back into the past of the women who had stood there; into the four-roomed houses of miners, into the homes of small shopkeepers and agricultural labourers, into the fields and factories of fifty or sixty years ago. Mrs Burrows, for example, had worked in the Lincolnshire fens when she was eight with forty or fifty other children, and an old man had followed the gang with a long whip in his hand 'which he did not forget to use'. That was a strange reflection. Most of the women had started work at seven or eight, earning a penny on Saturday for washing a doorstep, or twopence a week for carrying suppers to men at the iron foundry. They had gone into factories when they were fourteen. They had worked from seven in the morning till eight or nine at night and had made thirteen or fifteen shillings a week. Out of this money they had saved some pence with which to buy their mother gin – she was often very tired in the evening and had borne perhaps thirteen children in as many years; or they fetched opium to assuage some miserable old woman's ague in the fens. Old Betty Rollet killed herself when she could get no more. They had seen half-starved women standing in rows to be paid for their match-boxes while they snuffed the roast meat of their employer's dinner cooking within. The smallpox had raged in Bethnal Green and they had known that the boxes went on being made in the sick-room and were sold to the public with the infection still thick on them. They had been so cold working in the wintry fields that they could not run when the ganger gave them leave. They had waded through floods when the Wash overflowed its banks. Kind old ladies had given them parcels of food which had turned out to contain only crusts of bread and rancid bacon rind. All this they had done and seen and known when other children were still dabbling in seaside pools and spelling out fairy tales by the nursery fire. Naturally their faces had a different look on them. But they were, one remembered, firm faces, faces with something indomitable in their expression. Astonishing though it seems, human nature is so tough that it will take such wounds, even at the tenderest age, and survive them. Keep a child mewed in Bethnal Green and she will somehow snuff the country air from seeing the yellow dust on her brother's boots, and nothing will serve her but she must go there and see the 'clean ground', as she calls it, for herself. It was true that at first the 'bees were very frightening', but all the same she got to the country and the blue smoke and the cows came up to her expectation. Put girls, after a childhood of minding smaller brothers and washing door-steps, into a factory when they are fourteen and their eyes will turn to the window and they will be happy because, as the workroom is six storeys high, the sun can be seen breaking over the hills, 'and that was always such a comfort and help'. Still stranger, if one needs additional proof of the strength of the human instinct to escape from bondage and attach itself whether to a country road or to a sunrise over the hills, is the fact that the highest ideals of duty flourish in an obscure hat factory as surely as on a battlefield. There were women in Christies' felt hat factory, for example, who worked for 'honour'. They gave their lives to the cause of putting straight stitches into the bindings of men's hat brims. Felt is hard and thick; it is difficult to push the needle through; there are no rewards or glory to be won; but such is the incorrigible idealism of the human mind that there were 'trimmers' in those obscure places who would never put a crooked stitch in their work and ruthlessly tore out the crooked stitches of others. And as they drove in their straight stitches they reverenced Queen Victoria and thanked God, drawing up to the fire, that they were all married to good Conservative working men.

Certainly that story explained something of the force, of the obstinacy, which one had seen in the faces of the speakers at Newcastle. And then, if one went on reading these papers, one came upon other signs of the extraordinary vitality of the human spirit. That inborn energy which no amount of childbirth and washing up can quench had reached out, it seemed, and seized upon old copies of magazines; had attached itself to Dickens; had propped the poems of Burns against a dish cover to read while cooking. They read at meals; they read before going to the mill. They read Dickens and Scott and Henry George and Bulwer Lytton and Ella Wheeler Wilcox and Alice Meynell and would like 'to get hold of any good history of the French Revolution, not Carlyle's, please', and B. Russell on China, and William Morris and Shelley and Florence Barclay and Samuel Butler's Note Books – they read with the indiscriminate greed of a hungry appetite, that crams itself with toffee and beef and tarts and vinegar and champagne all in one gulp. Naturally such reading led to argument. The younger generation had the audacity to say that Queen

Victoria was no better than an honest charwoman who had brought up her children respectably. They had the temerity to doubt whether to sew straight stitches into men's hat brims should be the sole aim and end of a woman's life. They started arguments and even held rudimentary debating societies on the floor of the factory. In time the old trimmers even were shaken in their beliefs and came to think that there might be other ideals in the world besides straight stitches and Queen Victoria. Strange ideas indeed were seething in their brain. A girl, for instance, would reason, as she walked along the streets of a factory town, that she had no right to bring a child into the world if that child must earn its living in a mill. A chance saying in a book would fire her imagination to dream of future cities where there were to be baths and kitchens and washhouses and art galleries and museums and parks. The minds of working women were humming and their imaginations were awake. But how were they to realise their ideals? How were they to express their needs? It was hard enough for middle class women with some amount of money and some degree of education behind them. But how could women whose hands were full of work, whose kitchens were thick with steam, who had neither education nor encouragement nor leisure remodel the world according to the ideas of working women? It was then, I suppose, sometime in the eighties, that the Women's Guild crept modestly and tentatively into existence. For a time it occupied an inch or two of space in the *Co-operative News* which called itself The Women's Corner. It was there that Mrs Acland asked, 'Why should we not hold our Co-operative mothers' meetings, when we may bring our work and sit together, one of us reading some Co-operative work aloud, which may afterwards be discussed?' And on April 18th, 1883, she announced that the Women's Guild now numbered seven members. It was the Guild then that drew to itself all that restless wishing and dreaming. It was the Guild that made a central meeting place where formed and solidified all that was else so scattered and incoherent. The Guild must have given the older women, with their husbands and children, what 'clean ground' had given to the little girl in Bethnal Green, or the view of day breaking over the hills had given the girls in the hat factory. It gave them in the first place the rarest of all possessions − a room where they could sit down and think remote from boiling saucepans and crying children; and then that room became not merely a sitting-room and a meeting place, but a workshop where, laying their heads together, they could remodel their houses, could remodel their lives, could beat out this reform and that. And, as the membership grew, and twenty or thirty women made a practice of meeting weekly, so their ideas increased, and their interests widened. Instead of discussing merely their own taps and their own sinks and their own long hours and little pay, they began to discuss education and taxation and the conditions of work in the country at large. The women who had crept modestly in 1883 into Mrs Acland's sitting-room to sew and 'read some Co-operative work aloud', learnt to speak out, boldly and authoritatively, about every question of civic life. Thus it came about that Mrs Robson and Mrs Potter and Mrs Wright at Newcastle in 1913 were asking not only for baths and wages and electric light, but also for adult suffrage and the taxation of land values and divorce law reform. Thus in a year or two they were to demand peace and disarmament and the spread of Co-operative principles, not only among the working people of Great Britain, but among the nations of the world. And the force that lay behind their speeches and drove them home beyond the reach of eloquence was compact of many things – of men with whips, of sick-rooms where match-boxes were made, of hunger and cold, of many and difficult childbirths, of much scrubbing and washing up, of reading Shelley and William Morris and Samuel Butler over the kitchen table, of weekly meetings of the Women's Guild, of Committees and Congresses at Manchester and elsewhere. All this lay behind the speeches of Mrs Robson and Mrs Potter and Mrs Wright. The papers which you sent me certainly threw some light upon the old curiosities and bewilderments which had made that Congress so memorable, and so thick with unanswered questions.

But that the pages here printed should mean all this to those who cannot supplement the written word with the memory of faces and the sound of voices is perhaps unlikely. It cannot be denied that the chapters here put together do not make a book – that as literature they have many limitations. The writing, a literary critic might say, lacks detachment and imaginative breadth, even as the women themselves lacked variety and play of feature. Here are no reflections, he might object, no view of life as a whole, and no attempt to enter into the lives of other people. Poetry and fiction seem far beyond their horizon. Indeed, we are reminded of those obscure writers before the birth of Shakespeare who never travelled beyond the borders of their own parishes, who read no language but their own, and wrote with difficulty, finding few words and those awkwardly. And yet since writing is a complex art, much infected by life, these pages have some qualities even as literature that the literate and instructed might envy. Listen, for instance, to Mrs Scott, the felt hat worker: 'I have been over the hilltops when the snow drifts were over three feet high, and six feet in some places. I was in a blizzard in

Hayfield and thought I should never get round the corners. But it was life on the moors; I seemed to know every blade of grass and where the flowers grew and all the little streams were my companions.' Could she have said that better if Oxford had made her a Doctor of Letters? Or take Mrs Layton's description of a match-box factory in Bethnal Green and how she looked through the fence and saw three ladies 'sitting in the shade doing some kind of fancy work'. It has something of the accuracy and clarity of a description by Defoe. And when Mrs Burrows brings to mind that bitter day when the children were about to eat their cold dinner and drink their cold tea under the hedge and the ugly woman asked them into her parlour saying, 'Bring these children into my house and let them eat their dinner there,' the words are simple, but it is difficult to see how they could say more. And then there is a fragment of a letter from Miss Kidd — the sombre purple figure who typed as if the weight of the world were on her shoulders. 'When I was a girl of seventeen,' she writes, 'my then employer, a gentleman of good position and high standing in the town, sent me to his home one night, ostensibly to take a parcel of books, but really with a very different object. When I arrived at the house all the family were away, and before he would allow me to leave he forced me to yield to him. At eighteen I was a mother.' Whether that is literature or not literature I do not presume to say, but that it explains much and reveals much is certain. Such then was the burden that rested on that sombre figure as she sat typing your letters, such were the memories she brooded as she guarded your door with her grim and indomitable fidelity.

But I will quote no more. These pages are only fragments. These voices are beginning only now to emerge from silence into half articulate speech. These lives are still half hidden in profound obscurity. To express even what is expressed here has been a work of labour and difficulty. The writing has been done in kitchens, at odds and ends of leisure, in the midst of distractions and obstacles – but really there is no need for me, in a letter addressed to you, to lay stress upon the hardship of working women's lives. Have not you and Lilian Harris given your best years – but hush! you will not let me finish that sentence and therefore, with the old messages of friendship and admiration, I will make an end.

The Niece of an Earl

There is an aspect of fiction of so delicate a nature that less has been said about it than its importance deserves. One is supposed to pass over class distinctions in silence; one person is supposed to be as well born as another; and yet English fiction is so steeped in the ups and downs of social rank that without them it would be unrecognisable. When Meredith, in *The Case of General Ople and Lady Camper*, remarks, 'He sent word that he would wait on Lady Camper immediately, and betook himself forthwith to his toilette. She was the niece of an Earl', all of British blood accept the statement unhesitatingly, and know that Meredith is right. A General in those circumstances would certainly have given his coat an extra brush. For though the General might have been, we are given to understand that he was not, Lady Camper's social equal. He received the shock of her rank upon a naked surface. No earldom, baronetage, or knighthood protected him. He was an English gentleman merely, and a poor one at that. Therefore, to British readers even now it seems unquestionably fitting that he should 'betake himself to his toilette' before appearing in the lady's presence.

It is useless to suppose that social distinctions have vanished. Each may pretend that he knows no such restrictions, and that the compartment in which he lives allows

him the run of the world. But it is an illusion. The idlest
stroller down summer streets may see for himself the charwoman's shawl shouldering its way among the silk wraps
of the successful; he sees shop-girls pressing their noses
against the plate glass of motor-cars; he sees radiant youth
and august age waiting their summons within to be admitted
to the presence of King George. There is no animosity,
perhaps, but there is no communication. We are enclosed,
and separate, and cut off. Directly we see ourselves in the
looking-glass of fiction we know that this is so. The novelist,
and the English novelist in particular, knows and delights,
it seems, to know that Society is a nest of glass boxes one
separate from another, each housing a group with special
habits and qualities of its own. He knows that there are
Earls and that Earls have nieces; he knows that there are
Generals and that Generals brush their coats before they
visit the nieces of Earls. But this is only the A B C of what
he knows. For in a few short pages, Meredith makes us
aware not only that Earls have nieces, but that Generals
have cousins; that the cousins have friends; that the friends
have cooks; that the cooks have husbands, and that the
husbands of the cooks of the friends of the cousins of the
Generals are carpenters. Each of these people lives in a glass
box of his own, and has peculiarities of which the novelist
must take account. What appears superficially to be the vast
equality of the middle classes is, in truth, nothing of the
sort. All through the social mass run curious veins and
streakings separating man from man and woman from
woman; mysterious prerogatives and disabilities too ethereal
to be distinguished by anything so crude as a title impede
and disorder the great business of human intercourse. And
when we have threaded our way carefully through all these
grades from the niece of the Earl to the friend of the cousin

of the General, we are still faced with an abyss; a gulf yawns before us; on the other side are the working classes. The writer of perfect judgment and taste, like Jane Austen, does no more than glance across the gulf; she restricts herself to her own special class and finds infinite shades within it. But for the brisk, inquisitive, combative writer like Meredith, the temptation to explore is irresistible. He runs up and down the social scale; he chimes one note against another; he insists that the Earl and the cook, the General and the farmer shall speak up for themselves and play their part in the extremely complicated comedy of English civilised life.

It was natural that he should attempt it. A writer touched by the comic spirit relishes these distinctions keenly; they give him something to take hold of; something to make play with. English fiction without the nieces of Earls and the cousins of Generals would be an arid waste. It would resemble Russian fiction. It would have to fall back upon the immensity of the soul and upon the brotherhood of man. Like Russian fiction, it would lack comedy. But while we realise the immense debt that we owe the Earl's niece and the General's cousin, we doubt sometimes whether the pleasure we get from the play of satire on these broken edges is altogether worth the price we pay. For the price is a high one. The strain upon a novelist is tremendous. In two short stories Meredith gallantly attempts to bridge all gulfs, and to take half a dozen different levels in his stride. Now he speaks as an Earl's niece; now as a carpenter's wife. It cannot be said that his daring is altogether successful. One has a feeling (perhaps it is unfounded) that the blood of the niece of an Earl is not quite so tart and sharp as he would have it. Aristocracy is not, perhaps, so consistently high and brusque and eccentric as, from his angle, he would represent it. Yet his great people are more successful than his humble. His cooks are too ripe and rotund; his farmers too ruddy and earthy. He overdoes the pith and the sap; the fist-shaking and the thigh-slapping. He has got too far from them to write of them with ease.

It seems, therefore, that the novelist, and the English novelist in particular, suffers from a disability which affects no other artist to the same extent. His work is influenced by his birth. He is fated to know intimately, and so to describe with understanding, only those who are of his own social rank. He cannot escape from the box in which he has been bred. A bird's-eye view of fiction shows us no gentlemen in Dickens; no working men in Thackeray. One hesitates to call Jane Eyre a lady. The Elizabeths and the Emmas of Miss Austen could not possibly be taken for anything else. It is vain to look for dukes or for dustmen – we doubt that such extremes are to be found anywhere in fiction. We are, therefore, brought to the melancholy and tantalising conclusion not only that novels are poorer than they might be, but that we are very largely prevented – for after all, the novelists are the great interpreters – from knowing what is happening either in the heights of Society or in its depths. There is practically no evidence available by which we can guess at the feelings of the highest in the land. What does a King feel? What does a Duke think? We cannot say. For the highest in the land have seldom written at all, and have never written about themselves. We shall never know what the Court of Louis XIV looked like to Louis XIV himself. It seems likely indeed that the English aristocracy will pass out of existence, or be merged with the common people, without leaving any true picture of themselves behind.

But our ignorance of the aristocracy is nothing compared with our ignorance of the working classes. At all times the great families of England and France have delighted to have famous men at their tables, and thus the Thackerays and the Disraelis and the Prousts have been familiar enough with the cut and fashion of aristocratic life to write about it with authority. Unfortunately, however, life is so framed that literary success invariably means a rise, never a fall, and seldom, what is far more desirable, a spread in the social scale. The rising novelist is never pestered to come to gin and winkles with the plumber and his wife. His books never bring him into touch with the cat's-meat man, or start a correspondence with the old lady who sells matches and bootlaces by the gate of the British Museum. He becomes rich; he becomes respectable; he buys an evening suit and dines with peers. Therefore, the later works of successful novelists show, if anything, a slight rise in the social scale. We tend to get more and more portraits of the successful and the distinguished. On the other hand, the old rat-catchers and ostlers of Shakespeare's day are shuffled altogether off the scene, or become, what is far more offensive, objects of pity, examples of curiosity. They serve to show up the rich. They serve to point the evils of the social system. They are no longer, as they used to be when Chaucer wrote, simply themselves. For it is impossible, it would seem, for working men to write in their own language about their own lives. Such education as the act of writing implies at once makes them self-conscious, or class-conscious, or removes them from their own class. That anonymity, in the shadow of which writers write most happily, is the prerogative of the middle class alone. It is from the middle class that writers spring, because it is in the middle class only that the practice of writing is as natural and habitual as hoeing a field or building a house. Thus it must have been harder for Byron to be a poet than Keats;

and it is as impossible to imagine that a Duke could be a great novelist as that *Paradise Lost* could be written by a man behind a counter.

But things change; class distinctions were not always so hard and fast as they have now become. The Elizabethan age was far more elastic in this respect than our own; we, on the other hand, are far less hide-bound than the Victorians. Thus it may well be that we are on the edge of a greater change than any the world has yet known. In another century or so, none of these distinctions may hold good. The Duke and the agricultural labourer as we know them now may have died out as completely as the bustard and the wild cat. Only natural differences such as those of brain and character will serve to distinguish us. General Ople (if there are still Generals) will visit the niece (if there are still nieces) of the Earl (if there are still Earls) without brushing his coat (if there are still coats). But what will happen to English fiction when it has come to pass that there are neither Generals, nieces, Earls, nor coats, we cannot imagine. It may change its character so that we no longer know it. It may become extinct. Novels may be written as seldom and as unsuccessfully by our descendants as the poetic drama by ourselves. The art of a truly democratic age will be – what?

Lady Dorothy Nevill

She had stayed, in a humble capacity, for a week in the ducal household. She had seen the troops of highly decorated human beings descending in couples to eat, and ascending in couples to bed. She had, surreptitiously, from a gallery, observed the Duke himself dusting the miniatures in the glass cases, while the Duchess let her crochet fall from her hands as if in utter disbelief that the world had need of crochet. From an upper window she had seen, as far as eye could reach, gravel paths swerving round isles of greenery and losing themselves in little woods designed to shed the shade without the severity of forests; she had watched the ducal carriage bowling in and out of the prospect, and returning a different way from the way it went. And what was her verdict? 'A lunatic asylum.'

It is true that she was a lady's-maid, and that Lady Dorothy Nevill, had she encountered her on the stairs, would have made an opportunity to point out that that is a very different thing from being a lady.

> My mother never failed to point out the folly of work-women, shop-girls, and the like calling each other 'Ladies'. All this sort of thing seemed to her to be mere vulgar humbug, and she did not fail to say so.

What can we point out to Lady Dorothy Nevill? that with all her advantages she had never learned to spell? that she could not write a grammatical sentence? that she lived for eighty-seven years and did nothing but put food into her mouth and slip gold through her fingers? But delightful though it is to indulge in righteous indignation, it is misplaced if we agree with the lady's-maid that high birth is a form of congenital insanity, that the sufferer merely inherits the diseases of his ancestors, and endures them, for the most part very stoically, in one of those comfortably padded lunatic asylums which are known, euphemistically, as the stately homes of England.

Moreover, the Walpoles are not ducal. Horace Walpole's mother was a Miss Shorter; there is no mention of Lady Dorothy's mother in the present volume, but her great-grandmother was Mrs Oldfield the actress, and, to her credit, Lady Dorothy was 'exceedingly proud' of the fact. Thus she was not an extreme case of aristocracy; she was confined rather to a bird-cage than to an asylum; through the bars she saw people walking at large, and once or twice she made a surprising little flight into the open air. A gayer, brighter, more vivacious specimen of the caged tribe can seldom have existed; so that one is forced at times to ask whether what we call living in a cage is not the fate that wise people, condemned to a single sojourn upon earth, would choose. To be at large is, after all, to be shut out; to waste most of life in accumulating the money to buy and the time to enjoy what the Lady Dorothys find clustering and glowing about their cradles when their eyes first open – as hers opened in the year 1826 at number eleven Berkeley Square. Horace Walpole had lived there. Her father, Lord Orford, gambled it away in one night's play the year after she was born. But Wolterton Hall, in Norfolk, was full of carving and mantelpieces, and there were rare trees in the garden, and a large and famous lawn. No novelist could wish a more charming and even romantic environment in which to set the story of two little girls, growing up, wild yet secluded, reading Bossuet with their governess, and riding out on their ponies at the head of the tenantry on polling day. Nor can one deny that to have had the author of the following letter among one's ancestors would have been a source of inordinate pride. It is addressed to the Norwich Bible Society, which had invited Lord Orford to become its president:

> I have long been addicted to the Gaming Table. I have lately taken to the Turf. I fear I frequently blaspheme. But I have never distributed religious tracts. All this was known to you and your Society. Notwithstanding which you think me a fit person to be your president. God forgive your hypocrisy.

It was not Lord Orford who was in the cage on that occasion. But, alas! Lord Orford owned another country house, Ilsington Hall, in Dorsetshire, and there Lady Dorothy came in contact first with the mulberry tree, and later with Mr Thomas Hardy; and we get our first glimpse of the bars. We do not pretend to the ghost of an enthusiasm for Sailors' Homes in general; no doubt mulberry trees are much nicer to look at; but when it comes to calling people 'vandals' who cut them down to build houses, and to having footstools made from the wood, and to carving upon those footstools inscriptions which testify that 'often and often has King George III taken his tea' under this very footstool, then we want to protest – 'Surely you must mean Shakespeare?' But as her subsequent remarks upon Mr Hardy tend to prove, Lady Dorothy does not mean Shakespeare. She 'warmly appreciated' the works of Mr Hardy, and used to complain 'that the country families were too stupid to appreciate his genius at its proper worth'. George the Third drinking his tea; the county families failing to appreciate Mr Hardy: Lady Dorothy is undoubtedly behind the bars.

Yet no story more aptly illustrates the barrier which we perceive hereafter between Lady Dorothy and the outer world than the story of Charles Darwin and the blankets. Among her recreations Lady Dorothy made a hobby of growing orchids, and thus got into touch with 'the great naturalist'. Mrs Darwin, inviting her to stay with them, remarked with apparent simplicity that she had heard that people who moved much in London society were fond of being tossed in blankets. 'I am afraid,' her letter ended, 'we should hardly be able to offer you anything of that sort.' Whether in fact the necessity of tossing Lady Dorothy in a blanket had been seriously debated at Down, or whether Mrs Darwin obscurely hinted her sense of some incongruity between her husband and the lady of the orchids, we do not know. But we have a sense of two worlds in collision; and it is not the Darwin world that emerges in fragments. More and more do we see Lady Dorothy hopping from perch to perch, picking at groundsel here, and at hempseed there, indulging in exquisite trills and roulades, and sharpening her beak against a lump of sugar in a large, airy, magnificently equipped bird-cage. The cage was full of charming diversions. Now she illuminated leaves which had been macerated to skeletons; now she interested herself in improving the breed of donkeys; next she took up the cause of silkworms, almost threatened Australia with a plague of them, and 'actually succeeded in obtaining enough silk to make a dress'; again she was the first to discover that wood, gone green with decay, can be made, at some expense, into little boxes; she went into the question of funguses and established the virtues of the neglected English truffle; she imported rare fish; spent a great deal of energy in vainly trying to induce storks and Cornish choughs to breed in Sussex; painted on china; emblazoned heraldic arms, and, attaching whistles to the tails of pigeons, produced wonderful effects 'as of an aerial orchestra' when they flew through the air. To the Duchess of Somerset belongs the credit of investigating the proper way of cooking guinea-pigs; but Lady Dorothy was one of the first to serve up a dish of these little creatures at luncheon in Charles Street.

But all the time the door of the cage was ajar. Raids were made into what Mr Nevill calls 'Upper Bohemia'; from which Lady Dorothy returned with 'authors, journalists, actors, actresses, or other agreeable and amusing people'. Lady Dorothy's judgement is proved by the fact that they seldom misbehaved, and some indeed became quite domesticated, and wrote her 'very gracefully turned letters'. But once or twice, she made a flight beyond the cage herself. 'These horrors,' she said, alluding to the middle class, 'are so clever and we are so stupid; but then look how well they are educated, while our children learn nothing but how to spend their parents' money!' She brooded over the fact. Something was going wrong. She was too shrewd and too honest not to lay the blame partly at least upon her own class. 'I suppose she can just about read?' she said of one lady calling herself cultured; and of another, 'She is indeed curious and well adapted to open bazaars.' But to our thinking her most remarkable flight took place a year or two before her death, in the Victoria and Albert Museum:

I do so agree with you, [she wrote] – though I ought not

to say so – that the upper class are very – I don't know what to say – but they seem to take no interest in anything – but golfing, etc. One day I was at the Victoria and Albert Museum, just a few sprinkles of legs, for I am sure they looked too frivolous to have bodies and souls attached to them – but what softened the sight to my eyes were 2 little Japs poring over each article with a handbook . . . our bodies, of course, giggling and looking at nothing. Still worse, not one soul of the higher class visible: in fact I never heard of any one of them knowing of the place, and for this we are spending millions – it is all too painful.

It was all too painful, and the guillotine, she felt, loomed ahead. That catastrophe she was spared, for who could wish to cut off the head of a pigeon with a whistle attached to its tail? But if the whole bird-cage had been overturned and the aerial orchestra sent screaming and fluttering through the air, we can be sure, as Mr Joseph Chamberlain told her, that her conduct would have been 'a credit to the British aristocracy'.

'Queen Alexandra the Well-Beloved'

There can be no doubt that Queen Alexandra was an exquisitely pretty woman. Even the photographs in the present book put that beyond a doubt. Slim, upright, composed, one beautiful little hand clasped tenderly over a lap dog, the other controlling a perfect parasol, she drives through Rotten Row as, Miss Villiers would have us believe, she drove through the greater part of the nineteenth century. At the same time, she is completely dumb, and Miss Villiers is far too well-bred a courtier to break the Royal reserve. We are told nothing about her in the present little book except such facts as befit a lady with a lap dog. She was fond of sketching and music and children. Perhaps her most valuable contribution to her age was that she raised the standard of comfort for dogs. The kennels at Sandringham were famous, and the Queen attended to her pets with her own hands. Volumes, too, might be devoted to the gifts of chocolate boxes and dressing gowns, which descended from the sky, as if by miracle, upon the heads of ecstatic old men and women. But perhaps Miss Villiers' most valuable contribution to our knowledge of the Royal Family is the story she tells of a workman who found his way through a drain-pipe into Queen Mary's bedroom. She credits him with loyal motives – he wished to demonstrate, not to eavesdrop – and she recalls, what it is always pleasant to remember, the earlier exploits of the Boy Jones. For in writing the life of Queen Alexandra, it is frequently necessary to talk of something else.

Royalty

To begin with a quotation, since it may throw light upon a very, complex emotion: the accused came to town because, he said, 'I wanted to see the Dukes and Kings.'

The accused also said: 'The inner man tells me that I am a Duke.' Appearances were against him, and, as he had brought a pistol with him, his further actions took him to the Law Courts. But save that he went a step further than most of us, his state of mind was much the same as ours. We too want to see the Dukes and Kings. There is no denying it, for the picture papers show us what we want to see and the picture papers are full of Dukes and Kings. Even at times which it is sufficient to call 'like these' there are the little girls feeding the sea lions; there is the elderly lady accepting a bouquet; there is the young man with a ribbon across his breast. And we look at them, almost every day we look at them, because we too want to see the Dukes and Kings.

It is not a simple wish. It is very very old, to begin with, and old emotions like old families have intermarried and have many connections. Love of Royalty, or to give it its crude name, snobbery, is related to love of pageantry which has some connection with love of beauty – a respectable connection; and again with the imagination – which is still more respectable for it creates poems and novels. Certainly an old body in black with a pair of horn spectacles on her nose required a good deal of gilding by the imagination before she became the British Empire personified. Scott undoubtedly had to use the same imagination upon George the Fourth's tumbler to make it worth stealing that he had to use upon the Waverley Novels to make them worth reading. We must call up battles and banners and many ghosts and glories before we see whatever it is that we do see in the picture of a child feeding a bear with a bun. But perhaps the most profound satisfaction that Royalty provides is that it gives us a Paradise to inhabit, and one much more domestic than that provided by the Church of England. Pile carpets are more palpable than fields of asphodel, and the music of the Scots Grey more audible than the hymns angels play upon their harps. Moreover, real people live in Buckingham Palace, but always smiling, perfectly dressed, immune, we like to imagine, if not from death and sorrow, still from the humdrum and the pettifogging. Even though our inner man does not tell us that we are Dukes, it is a consolation to know that such beings exist. If they live, then we too live in them, vicariously. Probably most people, as they hold out a penny to the bus conductor on a rainy night, have caught themselves pretending that a beautiful lady is stooping to kiss the royal hand, and the omnibus is lit up.

The last few years, however, have done some damage to this great Victorian dream. For as we know, the Dukes and Kings refused to play their part in the game any longer. Two at least declared that they had hearts like ours; one heart loved a Smith, the other a Simpson. The danger of this admission was at once felt to be very great. A leading statesman foraged in the College of Heralds and discovered that the lady was descended, perhaps on the mother's side, perhaps from a Knight, who had perhaps fought at the Battle of Hastings. But the public was not to be bamboozled. We said, we cannot dream our dreams about people with hearts like ours. Such names as Smith and Simpson rouse us to reality. And the emotion was finely discriminated by a Court lady, who said that though she could curtsey to Queen Elizabeth, the pink of grace and charm, there was a difference – precisely what, she omitted to say – between the curtsey she dropped an Earl's daughter and the curtsey she gave Queen Mary the Royal. As for bending to a name which is to be read in large letters over a well-known shop in Piccadilly, her knees, she said, positively and, as it appeared, quite independently of their owner, refused to comply.

Enough has been said to show that the matter is complex. Further, blue blood by itself is not enough. For though there are extreme Royalists who can sustain themselves upon the shades of the Stuarts – do they not still come with their white roses to the Martyr's grave? – the cruder mass of us requires that Royalty shall have its crown and sceptre. In France for example there are princes of the Houses of Bourbon and Orleans whose blood is perhaps bluer than that of our own House of Windsor. But nobody cares to see them feeding pandas. No photographs of them appear in the French picture papers. Snobbery, it seems, can get no nourishment from the stout man in a frock coat, who is the present King of France, because he has lost his palace and his crown. It is like feeding upon a painted rose. Off it flits, this queer human sensibility, in search of other food.

Food it must have since it is alive and has been nourished, one way or another, ever since Hengist or

Horsa, many centuries ago some old tin vessel serve for a crown. In France, as every traveller knows, it has found a substitute. It feeds not upon Royalty but upon religion; not indeed upon those ardours and ecstasies which are the kernel, but upon the husks and pageantry. It feeds upon processions and images; upon wayside shrines; on the holy man in cloth of gold blessing the fishing-boat; on children in white muslin; on the penny candles and the incense. The Roman Catholic religion provides with this pageantry a substitute for Royalty. It gives the poorest old crone, who has nothing but a bunch of roses to stick in a pot, something to dream about, and, what is equally important, something to do.

The English religion, however, whether because of the climate because of the creed, has nothing of the kind to offer. It is a black and white indoor affair which makes no appeal to our senses and asks no help from our hands. If therefore Royalty fails to gratify our need of Royalty, the Protestant religion is not going to come to our help. The desire will have to find some other outlet. And the picture papers, in which we see the reflection of so many desires, are already hinting at a possible substitute. At present it is a hint only, and a very humble hint – nothing more than a caterpillar. It is true that it was a rare caterpillar; a gentleman in Kensington had found it in his back garden. And so it had its photograph in the news, and appeared almost life-size upon the very same page as the picture of the Princess who was feeding the panda. There they were, side by side. But what is important is that the eye, passing from the Princess to the caterpillar, registered a thrill which, though different from the Royalty thrill, was like enough to serve much the same purpose. The desire of the moth for the star; was gratified by the caterpillar. How wonderful

are caterpillars – so we may translate that thrill – symmetrical
in shape and brilliantly barred; the Privet Hawk wears, not
one garter ribbon across its breast, but three or four.
How little – the thrill continued – we know of the lives
of caterpillars, living mysteriously on the heights of elm
trees; urged by instincts that are not ours; immune from
worry; and capable, as we are not, of putting off this gross
body and winging their way . . . in short, the caterpillar
suggested that if a mere caterpillar found in Kensington
can cause this thrill (here curtailed) and if this thrill is much
the same as that which Royalty used to provide when
Royalty was barred and beautiful and immune from human
weakness, then perhaps Science will do instead. There is
in being, if at present only in germ, some curiosity about
this unknown world that might be fed. This unknown
world is after all more beautiful than Buckingham Palace,
and its inhabitants will never, in all probability, come down
from the tree-top to mate with the Smiths and the
Simpsons. If the picture papers then would come to our
help, we might dream a new dream, acquire a new
snobbery; we might see the coral insect at work; the panda
alone in his forest; the wild yet controlled dance of the
atoms which makes, it is said, the true being of the kitchen
table; and spend our curiosity upon them. The camera has
an immense power in its eye, if it would only turn that
eye in rather a different direction. It might wean us by
degrees from the Princess to the panda, and shunt us past
religion to pay homage to Science, as some think a more
venerable royal house than the House of Windsor. Above
all it could check the most insidious and dangerous of
current snob-beries, which is making the workers into
Kings; has invested the slum, the mine, and the factory
with the old glamour of the palace, so that, as modem

fiction shows, we are beginning to escape, by picturing the lives of the poor and day dreaming about them, from the drudgery, about which there is no sort of glamour, of being ourselves.

Lives of the Obscure

Dr Bentley

As we saunter through those famous courts where Dr Bentley once reigned supreme we sometimes catch sight of a figure hurrying on its way to Chapel or Hall which, as it disappears, draws our thoughts enthusiastically after it. For that man, we are told, has the whole of Sophocles at his finger-ends; knows Homer by heart; reads Pindar as we read *The Times*; and spends his life, save for these short excursions to eat and pray, wholly in the company of the Greeks. It is true that the infirmities of our education prevent us from appreciating his emendations as they deserve; his life's work is a sealed book to us; none the less, we treasure up the last flicker of his black gown, and feel as if a bird of Paradise had flashed by us, so bright is his spirit's raiment, and in the murk of a November evening we had been privileged to see it winging its way to roost in fields of amaranth and beds of moly. Of all men, great scholars are the most mysterious, the most august. Since it is unlikely that we shall ever be admitted to their intimacy, or see much more of them than a black gown crossing a court at dusk, the best we can do is to read their lives – for example, the *Life of Dr. Bentley* by Bishop Monk.

There we shall find much that is odd and little that is reassuring. The greatest of our scholars, the man who read Greek as the most expert of us read English not merely with an accurate sense of meaning and grammar but with a sensibility so subtle and widespread that he perceived relations and suggestions of language which enabled him to fetch up from oblivion lost lines and inspire new life into the little fragments that remained, the man who should have been steeped in beauty (if what they say of the Classics is true) as a honey-pot is ingrained with sweetness was, on the contrary, the most quarrelsome of mankind.

'I presume that there are not many examples of an individual who has been a party in six distinct suits before the Court of King's Bench within the space of three years', his biographer remarks; and adds that Bentley won them all. It is difficult to deny his conclusion that though Dr Bentley might have been a first-rate lawyer or a great soldier 'such a display suited any character rather than that of a learned and dignified clergyman'. Not all these disputes, however, sprung from his love of literature. The charges against which he had to defend himself were directed against him as Master of Trinity College, Cambridge. He was habitually absent from chapel; his expenditure upon building and upon his household was excessive; he used the college seal at meetings which did not consist of the statutable number of sixteen, and so on. In short, the career of the Master of Trinity was one continuous series of acts of aggression and defiance, in which Dr Bentley treated the Society of Trinity College as a grown man might treat an importunate rabble of street boys. Did they dare to hint that the staircase at the Lodge which admitted four persons abreast was quite wide enough? – did they refuse to sanction his expenditure upon a new one? Meeting them in the Great Court one evening after chapel he proceeded urbanely to question them. They refused to budge. Whereupon, with a sudden alteration of colour and voice, Bentley demanded whether 'they had forgotten his rusty sword?' Mr Michael Hutchinson and some others, upon whose backs the weight of that weapon would have first descended, brought pressure upon their seniors. The bill for £350 was paid and their preferment secured. But Bentley did not wait for this act of submission to finish his staircase.

So it went on, year after year. Nor was the arrogance of his behaviour always justified by the splendour or utility of the objects he had in view – the creation of the Backs, the erection of an observatory, the foundation of a laboratory. More trivial desires were gratified with the same tyranny. Sometimes he wanted coal; sometimes bread and ale; and then Madame Bentley, sending her servant with a snuff-box in token of authority, got from the butteries at the expense of the college a great deal more of these commodities than the college thought that Dr Bentley ought to require. Again, when he had four pupils to lodge with him who paid him handsomely for their board, it was drawn from the College, at the command of the snuff-box, for nothing. The principles of 'delicacy and good feeling' which the Master might have been expected to observe (great scholar as he was, steeped in the wine of the Classics) went for nothing. His argument that the 'few College loaves' upon which the four young patricians were nourished were amply repaid by the three sash windows which he had put into their rooms at his own expense failed to convince the Fellows. And when, on Trinity Sunday 1719, the Fellows found the famous College ale not to their liking, they were scarcely satisfied when the butler told them that it had been brewed by the Master's orders, from the Master's malt, which was stored in the Master's granary, and though damaged by 'an insect called the weevil' had been paid for at the very high rates which the Master demanded.

Still these battles over bread and beer are trifles and domestic trifles at that. His conduct in his profession will throw more light upon our inquiry. For, released from brick and building, bread and beer, patricians and their windows, it may be found that he expanded in the atmosphere of Homer, Horace, and Manilius, and proved in his study the benign nature of those influences which have been wafted down to us through the ages. But there the evidence is even less to the credit of the dead languages. He acquitted himself magnificently, all agree, in the great controversy about the letters of Phalaris. His temper was excellent and his learning prodigious. But that triumph was succeeded by a series of disputes which force upon us the extraordinary spectacle of men of learning and genius, of authority and divinity, brawling about Greek and Latin texts, and calling each other names for all the world like bookies on a racecourse or washerwomen in a back street. For this vehemence of temper and virulence of language were not confined to Bentley alone; they appear unhappily characteristic of the profession as a whole. Early in life, in the year 1691, a quarrel was fastened upon him by his brother chaplain Hody for writing Malelas, not as Hody preferred, Malela. A controversy in which Bentley displayed learning and wit, and Hody accumulated endless pages of bitter argument against the letter s ensued. Hody was worsted, and 'there is too much reason to believe, that the offence given by this trivial cause was never afterwards healed'. Indeed, to mend a line was to break a friendship. James Gronovius of Leyden – 'homunculus eruditione mediocri, ingenio nullo', as Bentley called him – attacked Bentley for ten years because Bentley had succeeded in correcting a fragment of Callimachus where he had failed.

But Gronovius was by no means the only scholar who

resented the success of a rival with a rancour that grey hairs and forty years spent in editing the Classics failed to subdue. In all the chief towns of Europe lived men like the notorious de Pauw of Utrecht, 'a person who has justly been considered the pest and disgrace of letters', who, when a new theory or new edition appeared, banded themselves together to deride and humiliate the scholar. '. . . all his writings,' Bishop Monk remarks of de Pauw, 'prove him to be devoid of candour, good faith, good manners, and every gentlemanly feeling: and while he unites all the defects and bad qualities that were ever found in a critic or commentator, he adds one peculiar to himself, an incessant propensity to indecent allusions.' With such tempers and such habits it is not strange that the scholars of those days sometimes ended lives made intolerable by bitterness, poverty, and neglect by their own hands, like Johnson, who after a lifetime spent in the detection of minute errors of construction, went mad and drowned himself in the meadows near Nottingham. On May 20, 1712, Trinity College was shocked to find that the professor of Hebrew, Dr Sike, had hanged himself 'some time this evening, before candlelight, in his sash'. When Kuster died, it was reported that he, too, had killed himself. And so, in a sense, he had. For when his body was opened 'there was found a cake of sand along the lower region of his belly. This, I take it, was occasioned by his sitting nearly double, and writing on a very low table, surrounded with three or four circles of books placed on the ground, which was the situation we usually found him in.' The minds of poor schoolmasters like John Ker of the dissenting Academy, who had had the high gratification of dining with Dr Bentley at the Lodge, when the talk fell upon the use of the word *equidem*, were so distorted by a lifetime of neglect and study that they went home, collected all uses of the word *equidem* which contradicted the Doctor's opinion, returned to the Lodge, anticipating in their simplicity a warm welcome, met the Doctor issuing to dine with the Archbishop of Canterbury, followed him down the street in spite of his indifference and annoyance and, being refused even a word of farewell, went home to brood over their injuries and wait the day of revenge.

But the bickerings and animosities of the smaller fry were magnified, not obliterated, by the Doctor himself in the conduct of his own affairs. The courtesy and good temper which he had shown in his early controversies had worn away. '. . . a course of violent animosities and the indulgence of unrestrained indignation for many years had impaired both his taste and judgement in controversy', and he condescended, though the subject in dispute was the Greek Testament, to call his antagonist 'maggot', 'vermin', 'gnawing rat', and 'cabbage head', to refer to the darkness of his complexion, and to insinuate that his wits were crazed, which charge he supported by dwelling on the fact that his brother, a clergyman, wore a beard to his girdle.

Violent, pugnacious, and unscrupulous, Dr Bentley survived these storms and agitations, and remained, though suspended from his degrees and deprived of his mastership, seated at the Lodge imperturbably. Wearing a broad-brimmed hat indoors to protect his eyes, smoking his pipe, enjoying his port, and expounding to his friends his doctrine of the digamma, Bentley lived those eighty years which, he said, were long enough 'to read everything which was worth reading', 'Et tunc', he added, in his peculiar manner,

Et tunc magna mei sub terris ibit imago.

A small square stone marked his grave in Trinity College, but the Fellows refused to record upon it the fact that he had been their Master.

But the strangest sentence in this strange story has yet to be written, and Bishop Monk writes it as if it were a commonplace requiring no comment. 'For a person who was neither a poet, nor possessed of poetical taste to venture upon such a task was no common presumption.' The task was to detect every slip of language in *Paradise Lost*, and all instances of bad taste and incorrect imagery. The result was notoriously lamentable. Yet in what, we may ask, did it differ from those in which Bentley was held to have acquitted himself magnificently? And if Bentley was incapable of appreciating the poetry of Milton, how can we accept his verdict upon Horace and Homer? And if we cannot trust implicitly to scholars, and if the study of Greek is supposed to refine the manners and purify the soul – but enough. Our scholar has returned from Hall; his lamp is lit; his studies are resumed; and it is time that our profane speculations should have an end. Besides, all this happened many, many years ago.

Laetitia Pilkington

Let us bother the librarian once again. Let us ask him to reach down, dust, and hand over to us that little brown book over there, the *Memoirs of Mrs. Pilkington*, three volumes bound in one, printed by Peter Hoey in Dublin, MDCCLXXVI. The deepest obscurity shades her retreat; the dust lies heavy on her tomb – one board is loose, that is to say, and nobody has read her since early in the last century when a reader, presumably a lady, whether disgusted by her obscenity or stricken by the hand of death, left off in the middle and marked her place with a faded list of goods and groceries. If ever a woman wanted a champion, it is obviously Laetitia Pilkington. Who then was she?

Can you imagine a very extraordinary cross between Moll Flanders and Lady Ritchie, between a rolling and rollicking woman of the town and a lady of breeding and refinement? Laetitia Pilkington (1712–1759) was something of the sort – shady, shifty, adventurous, and yet, like Thackeray's daughter, like Miss Mitford, like Madame de Sévigné and Jane Austen and Maria Edgeworth, so imbued with the old traditions of her sex that she wrote, as ladies talk, to give pleasure. Throughout her *Memoirs*, we can never forget that it is her wish to entertain, her unhappy fate to sob. Dabbing her eyes and controlling her anguish, she begs us to forgive an odious breach of manners which only the suffering of a lifetime, the intolerable persecutions of Mr P——n, the malignant, she must say the h——h, spite of Lady C——t can excuse. For who should know better than the Earl of Killmallock's great-granddaughter that it is the part of a lady to hide her sufferings? Thus Laetitia is in the great tradition of English women of letters. It is her duty to entertain; it is her instinct to conceal. Still, though her room near the Royal Exchange is threadbare, and the table is spread with old play-bills instead of a cloth, and the butter is served in a shoe, and Mr Worsdale has used the teapot to fetch small beer that very morning, still she presides, still she entertains. Her language is a trifle coarse, perhaps. But who taught her English? The great Doctor Swift.

In all her wanderings, which were many, and in her failings, which were great, she looked back to those early Irish days when Swift had pinched her into propriety of speech. He had beaten her for fumbling at a drawer: he had daubed her cheeks with burnt cork to try her temper; he had bade her pull off her shoes and stockings and stand against the wainscot and let him measure her. At first she had refused; then she had yielded. 'Why,' said the Dean, 'I suspected you had either broken Stockings or foul toes, and in either case should have delighted to expose you.' Three feet two inches was all she measured, he declared, though, as Laetitia complained, the weight of Swift's hand on her head had made her shrink to half her size. But she was foolish to complain. Probably she owed her intimacy to that very fact – she was only three feet two. Swift had lived a lifetime among the giants; now there was a charm in dwarfs. He took the little creature into his library. '"Well," said he, "I have brought you here to show you all the Money I got when I was in the Ministry, but don't steal any of it." "I won't, indeed, Sir," said I; so he opened a Cabinet, and showed me a whole parcel of empty drawers. "Bless me," says he, "the Money is flown.'" There was a charm in her surprise; there was a charm in her humility. He could beat her and bully her, make her shout when he was deaf, force her husband to drink the lees of the wine, pay their cab fares, stuff guineas into a piece of gingerbread, and relent surprisingly, as if there were something grimly pleasing to him in the thought of so foolish a midget setting up to have a life and a mind of her own. For with Swift she was herself; it was the effect of his genius. She had to pull off the stockings if he told her to. So, though his satire terrified her, and she found it highly unpleasant to dine at the Deanery and see him watching, in the great glass which hung before him for that purpose, the butler stealing beer at the sideboard, she knew that it was a privilege to walk with him in his garden; to hear him talk of Mr Pope and quote Hudibras; and then be hustled back in the rain to save coach hire, and then to sit chatting in the parlour with Mrs Brent, the housekeeper, about the Dean's oddity and charity, and how the sixpence he saved on the coach he gave to the lame old man who sold gingerbread at the corner, while the Dean dashed up the front stairs and down the back so violently that she was afraid he would fall and hurt himself.

But memories of great men are no infallible specific. They fall upon the race of life like beams from a lighthouse. They flash, they shock, they reveal, they vanish. To remember Swift was of little avail to Laetitia when the troubles of life came thick about her. Mr Pilkington left her for Widow W—rr—n. Her father – her dear father – died. The sheriff's officers insulted her. She was deserted in an empty house with two children to provide for. The tea chest was secured, the garden gate locked, and the bills left unpaid. And still she was young and attractive and gay, with an inordinate passion for scribbling verses and an incredible hunger for reading books. It was this that was her undoing. The book was fascinating and the hour late. The gentleman would not lend it, but would stay till she had finished. They sat in her bedroom. It was highly indiscreet, she owned. Suddenly twelve watchmen broke through the kitchen window, and Mr Pilkington appeared with a cambric handkerchief tied about his neck. Swords were drawn and heads broken. As for her excuse, how could one expect Mr Pilkington and the twelve watchmen to believe this? Only reading! Only sitting up late to finish a new book! Mr Pilkington and the watchmen interpreted the situation as such men would. But lovers of learning, she is persuaded, will understand her passion and deplore its consequences.

And now what was she to do? Reading had played her false, but still she could write. Ever since she could form her letters, indeed, she had written with incredible speed and considerable grace, odes, addresses, apostrophes to Miss Hoadley, to the Recorder of Dublin, to Dr Delany's place in the country. 'Hail, happy Delville, blissful seat!' 'Is there a man whose fixed and steady gaze —' the verses flowed without the slightest difficulty on the slightest occasion. Now, therefore, crossing to England, she set up, as her advertisement had it, to write letters upon any subject, except the law, for twelve pence ready money, and no trust given. She lodged opposite White's Chocolate House, and there, in the evening, as she watered her flowers on the leads the noble gentlemen in the window across the road drank her health, sent her over a bottle of burgundy; and later she heard old Colonel —— crying, 'Poke after me, my lord, poke after me,' as he shepherded the D—— of M—lb—gh up her dark stairs. That lovely gentleman, who honoured his title by wearing it, kissed her, complimented her, opened his pocket-book, and left her with a bank-note for fifty pounds upon Sir Francis Child. Such tributes stimulated her pen to astonishing outbursts of impromptu gratitude. If, on the other hand, a gentleman refused to buy or a lady hinted impropriety, this same flowery pen writhed and twisted in agonies of hate and vituperation. 'Had I said that your F——r died Blaspheming the Almighty,' one of her accusations begins, but the end is unprintable. Great ladies were accused of every depravity, and the clergy, unless their taste in poetry was above reproach, suffered an incessant castigation. Mr Pilkington, she never forgot, was a clergyman.

Slowly but surely the Earl of Killmallock's great-granddaughter descended in the social scale. From St James's Street and its noble benefactors she migrated to Green Street to lodge with Lord Stair's *valet de chamber* and his wife, who washed for persons of distinction. She, who had dallied with dukes, was glad for company's sake to take a hand at quadrille with footmen and laundresses and Grub Street writers, who, as they drank porter, sipped green tea, and smoked tobacco, told stories of the utmost scurrility about their masters and mistresses. The spiciness of their conversation made amends for the vulgarity of their manners. From them Laetitia picked up those anecdotes of the great which sprinkled her pages with dashes and served her purpose when subscribers failed and landladies grew insolent. Indeed, it was a hard life – to trudge to Chelsea in the snow wearing nothing but a chintz gown and be put off with a beggarly half-crown by Sir Hans Sloane; next to tramp to Ormond Street and extract two guineas from the odious Dr Meade, which, in her glee, she tossed in the air and lost in a crack of the floor; to be insulted by footmen; to sit down to a dish of boiling water because her landlady must not guess that a pinch of tea was beyond her means. Twice on moonlight nights, with the lime trees in flower, she wandered in St James's Park and contemplated suicide in Rosamond's Pond. Once, musing among the tombs in Westminster Abbey, the door was locked on her, and she had to spend the night in the pulpit wrapped in a carpet from the Communion Table to protect herself from the assaults of rats. 'I long to listen to the young-ey'd cherubims!' she exclaimed. But a very different fate was in store for her. In spite of Mr Colley Cibber, and Mr Richardson, who supplied her first with gilt-edged notepaper and then with baby linen, those harpies, her landladies, after drinking her ale, devouring her lobsters, and failing often for years at a time to comb their hair, succeeded in driving Swift's friend, and the Earl's great-granddaughter, to be imprisoned with common debtors in the Marshalsea.

Bitterly she cursed her husband, who had made her a lady of adventure instead of what nature intended, 'a harmless household dove'. More and more wildly she ransacked her brains for anecdotes, memories, scandals, views about the bottomless nature of the sea, the inflammable character of the earth – anything that would fill a page and earn her a guinea. She remembered that she had eaten plovers' eggs with Swift. 'Here, Hussey,' said he, 'is a Plover's egg. King William used to give crowns apiece for them . . .' Swift never laughed, she remembered. He used to suck in his cheeks instead of laughing. And what else could she remember? A great many gentlemen, a great many landladies; how the window was thrown up when her father died, and her sister came downstairs, with the sugar-basin, laughing. All had been bitterness and struggle, except that she had loved

Shakespeare, known Swift, and kept through all the shifts and shades of an adventurous career a gay spirit, something of a lady's breeding, and the gallantry which, at the end of her short life, led her to crack her joke and enjoy her duck with death at her heart and duns at her pillow.

Jones and Wilkinson

Whether Jones should come before Wilkinson or Wilkinson before Jones is not a matter likely to agitate many breasts at the present moment, seeing that more than a hundred and fifty years have rolled over the gentlemen in question and diminished a lustre which, even in their own time, round about the year 1750, was not very bright. The Rev. Dr Wilkinson might indeed claim precedence by virtue of his office. He was His Majesty's Chaplain of the Savoy and Chaplain also to his late Royal Highness, Frederick Prince of Wales. But then Dr Wilkinson was transported. Captain James Jones might assert that, as Captain of His Majesty's third regiment of Guards with a residence by virtue of his office in Savoy Square, his social position was equal to the Doctor's. But Captain Jones had to seclude himself beyond the reach of the law at Mortlake. What, however, renders these comparisons peculiarly odious is the fact that the Captain and the Doctor were boon companions whose tastes were congenial, whose incomes were insufficient, whose wives drank tea together, and whose houses in the Savoy were not two hundred yards apart. Dr Wilkinson, for all his sacred offices (he was Rector of Coyty in Glamorgan, stipendiary curate of Wise in Kent, and, through Lord Galway, had the right to 'open plaister-pits in the honour of Pontefract'), was a convivial spirit who cut a splendid figure in the pulpit, preached and read prayers in a voice that was clear, strong and sonorous so that many a lady of fashion never 'missed her pew near the pulpit', and persons of title remembered him many years after misfortune had removed the handsome preacher from their sight.

Captain Jones shared many of his friend's qualities. He was vivacious, witty, and generous, well made and elegant in person, and, if he was not quite as handsome as the doctor, he was perhaps rather his superior in intellect. Compare them as we may, however, there can be little doubt that the gifts and tastes of both gentlemen were better adapted for pleasure than for labour, for society than for solitude, for the hazards and pleasures of the table rather than for the rigours of religion and war. It was the gaming-table that seduced Captain Jones, and here, alas, his gifts and graces stood him in little stead. His affairs became more and more hopelessly embarrassed, so that shortly, instead of being able to take his walks at large, he was forced to limit them to the precincts of St James's, where, by ancient prerogative, such unfortunates as he were free from the attentions of the bailiffs.

To so gregarious a spirit the confinement was irksome. His only resource, indeed, was to get into talk with any such 'park-saunterers' as misfortunes like his own had driven to perambulate the Park, or, when the weather allowed, to bask and loiter and gossip on its benches. As chance would have it (and the Captain was a devotee of that goddess) he found himself one day resting on the same bench with an elderly gentleman of military aspect and stern demeanour, whose ill-temper the wit and humour which all allowed to Captain Jones presumably beguiled, so that whenever the Captain appeared in the Park, the old man sought his company, and they passed the time until dinner very pleasantly in talk. On no occasion, however, did the General – for it appeared that the name of this morose old man was General Skelton – ask Captain Jones to his house; the acquaintance went no further than the bench in St James's Park; and when, as soon fell out, the Captain's difficulties forced him to the greater privacy of a little cabin at Mortlake, he forgot entirely the military gentleman who, presumably, still sought an appetite for dinner or some alleviation of his own sour mood in loitering and gossiping with the park-saunterers of St James's.

But among the amiable characteristics of Captain Jones was a love of wife and child, scarcely to be wondered at, indeed, considering his wife's lively and entertaining dis-position and the extraordinary promise of that little girl who was later to become the wife of Lord Cornwallis. At whatever risk to himself, Captain Jones would steal back to revisit his wife and to hear his little girl recite the part of Juliet which, under his teaching, she had perfectly by heart. On one such secret journey he was hurrying to get within the royal sanctuary of St James's when a voice called on him to stop. His fears obsessing him, he hurried the faster, his pursuer close at his heels. Realising that escape was impossible, Jones wheeled about and facing his pursuer, whom he recognised as the Attorney Brown, demanded what his enemy wanted of him. Far from being his enemy, said Brown, he was the best friend he had ever had, which he would prove if Jones would accompany him to the first tavern that came to hand. There, in a private room over a fire, Mr Brown disclosed the following astonishing story. An unknown friend, he said, who had scrutinised Jones's conduct carefully and concluded that his deserts outweighed his misdemeanours, was prepared to settle all his debts and indeed to put him beyond the reach of such tormentors in future. At these words a load was lifted from Jones's heart, and he cried out 'Good God! Who can this paragon of friendship be?' It was none other, said Brown, than General Skelton. General Skelton, the man whom he had only met to chat with on a bench in St James's Park? Jones asked in wonderment. Yes, it was the General, Brown assured him. Then let him hasten to throw himself in gratitude at his benefactor's knee! Not so fast, Brown replied; General Skelton will never speak to you again. General Skelton died last night.

The extent of Captain Jones's good fortune was indeed magnificent. The General had left Captain Jones sole heir to all his possessions on no other condition than that he should assume the name of Skelton instead of Jones. Hastening through streets no longer dreadful, since every debt of honour could now be paid, Captain Jones brought his wife the astonishing news of their good fortune, and they promptly set out to view that part which lay nearest to hand – the General's great house in Henrietta Street. Gazing about her, half in dream, half in earnest, Mrs Jones was so overcome with the tumult of her emotions that she could not stay to gather in the extent of her possessions, but ran to Little Bedford Street, where Mrs Wilkinson was then living, to impart her joy. Meanwhile, the news that General Skelton lay dead in Henrietta Street without a son to succeed him spread abroad, and those who thought themselves his heirs arrived in the house of death to take stock of their inheritance, among them one great and beautiful lady whose avarice was her undoing, whose misfortunes were equal to her sins, Kitty Chudleigh, Countess of Bristol, Duchess of Kingston. Miss Chudleigh, as she then called herself, believed, and who can doubt that with her passionate nature, her lust for wealth and property, her pistols and her parsimony, she believed with vehemence and asserted her belief with arrogance, that all General Skelton's property had legally descended to her. Later, when the will was read and the truth made public that not only the house in Henrietta Street, but Pap Castle in Cumberland and the lands and lead mines pertaining to it, were left without exception to an unknown Captain Jones, she burst out in 'terms exceeding all bounds of delicacy'. She cried that her relative the General was an old fool in his dotage, that Jones and his wife were impudent low upstarts beneath her notice, and so flounced into her coach 'with a scornful quality toss' to carry on that life of deceit and intrigue and ambition which drove her later to wander in ignominy, an outcast from her country.

What remains to be told of the fortunes of Captain Jones can be briefly despatched. Having new furnished the house in Henrietta Street, the Jones family set out when summer came to visit their estates in Cumberland. The country was so fair, the Castle so stately, the thought that now all belonged to them so gratifying that their progress for three weeks was one of unmixed pleasure and the spot where they were now to live seemed a paradise. But there was an eagerness, an impetuosity about James Jones which made him impatient to suffer even the smiles of fortune passively. He must be active – he must be up and doing. He must be 'let down', for all his friends could do to dissuade him, to view a lead mine. The consequences as they foretold were disastrous. He was drawn up, indeed, but already infected with a deadly sickness of which in a few days he died, in the arms of his wife, in the midst of that paradise which he had toiled so long to reach and now was to die without enjoying.

Meanwhile the Wilkinsons – but that name, alas, was no

longer applicable to them, nor did the Doctor and his wife any more inhabit the house in the Savoy – the Wilkinsons had suffered more extremities at the hands of Fate than the Joneses themselves. Dr Wilkinson, it has been said, resembled his friend Jones in the conviviality of his habits and his inability to keep within the limits of his income. Indeed, his wife's dowry of two thousand pounds had gone to pay off the debts of his youth. But by what means could he pay off the debts of his middle age? He was now past fifty, and what with good company and good living, was seldom free from duns, and always pressed for money. Suddenly, from an unexpected quarter, help appeared. This was none other than the Marriage Act, passed in 1755, which laid it down that if any person solemnised a marriage without publishing the banns, unless a marriage licence had already been obtained, he should be subject to transportation for fourteen years. Dr Wilkinson, looking at the matter, it is to be feared, from his own angle, and with a view to his own necessities, argued that as Chaplain of the Savoy, which was extra-Parochial and Royal-exempt, he could grant licences as usual – a privilege which at once brought him such a glut of business, such a crowd of couples wishing to be married in a hurry, that the rat-tat-tat never ceased on his street door, and cash flooded the family exchequer so that even his little boy's pockets were lined with gold. The duns were paid; the table sumptuously spread. But Dr Wilkinson shared another failing with his friend Jones; he would not take advice. His friends warned him; the Government plainly hinted that if he persisted they would be forced to act. Secure in what he imagined to be his right, enjoying the prosperity it brought him to the full, the Doctor paid no heed. On Easter Day he was engaged in marrying from eight in the morning till twelve at night.

At last, one Sunday, the King's Messengers appeared. The Doctor escaped by a secret walk over the leads of the Savoy, made his way to the river bank, where he slipped upon some logs and fell, heavy and elderly as he was, in the mud; but nevertheless got to Somerset stairs, took a boat, and reached the Kentish shore in safety. Even now he brazened it out that the law was on his side, and came back four weeks later prepared to stand his trial. Once more, for the last time, company overflowed the house in the Savoy; lawyers abounded, and, as they ate and drank, assured Dr Wilkinson that his case was already won. In July 1756 the trial began. But what conclusion could there be? The crime had been committed and persisted in openly in spite of warning. The Doctor was found guilty and sentenced to fourteen years' transportation.

It remained for his friends to fit him out, like the gentleman he was, for his voyage to America. There, they argued, his gifts of speech and person would make him welcome, and later his wife and son could join him. To them he bade farewell in the dismal precincts of Newgate in March 1757. But contrary winds beat the ship back to shore; the gout seized on a body enfeebled by pleasure and adversity; at Plymouth Dr Wilkinson was transported finally and for ever. The lead mine undid Jones; the Marriage Act was the downfall of Wilkinson. Both now sleep in peace, Jones in Cumberland, Wilkinson, far from his friend (and if their failings were great, great too were their gifts and graces) on the shores of the melancholy Atlantic.

All About Books

Your last letter ends with the following sentence: 'The cold profile of Mont Blanc; falling snow; peasants and pine trees; a string of stout fellows roped together with alpenstocks – such is the prospect from my window; so for pity's sake draw your chair to the fire, take your pen in your hand and write me a long, long letter all about books.' But you must realise that a long, long letter is apt to be exaggerated, inaccurate, and full of those irreticences and hyperboles which the voice of the speaker corrects in talk. A letter is not a review; it is not a considered judgment, but, on condition that you do not believe a word I say, I will scribble for an hour or two whatever comes into my head about books.

That it has been a very bad season goes without saying. The proof of it is that old Mr Baddeley had read *Guy Mannering* for the fifty-eighth time. Never was Jane Austen in greater demand. Trollope, Dickens, Carlyle and Macaulay are all providing that solace, that security, that sense that the human heart does not change which our miserable age requires and our living authors so woefully fail to provide. When, therefore, the rumour spread that the diary of an old clergyman called Cole, who had gone to Paris in the autumn of 1765, was about to be published, and that Miss Waddell had put her brilliance and her erudition at our service, a purr of content and anticipation rose from half the arm-chairs of England. This Cole, moreover, was not anybody's Cole; he was Horace Walpole's Cole; nor does it need any pedantic familiarity with history to be aware that the autumn of 1765 was for one old blind woman in Paris the most excruciating, the most humiliating, the most ecstatic of her life. At last Horace Walpole had come – after what snubs, what humiliations, what bitter disappointments! At last Madame du Deffand would – not indeed see him in the flesh, but feel him with the spirit. He would be in the same room with her; he would talk his broken French; she would feel come over her that strange delight, that abasement, that ecstasy – call it not love, for love he would not have it called – which the presence of the elderly and elegant Horace never failed to inspire in a heart that had long out-lived any sensation but boredom, despair and disgust. It was in that very autumn that Cole chose to visit Paris. Cole, it seemed probable since Walpole liked him, would have eyes in his head; certainly he had a diary in his portmanteau. What revelations might one not expect? What confidences from one Englishman to another? And Horace Walpole was willing. Every day he sent his servant to ask Cole to dinner. And every day – it is incredible what the dead will do, but it is true – Cole preferred to go sightseeing. He went to Notre Dame; he went to the Sorbonne; he went to the Convent of that Virgin, to the Cathedral of this Saint. When he came home he sat down to digest and methodise what he had seen. He was too tired to dine with Mr Walpole. So instead of revelations we have information. 'On the right hand of the High Altar as one enters. . . . The dome of this church is very beautiful. . . . Over the door is a curious alto-relievo representing the Last Supper. . . .' That is what he writes about, and, of course, about the habits of the natives. The habits of the natives are disgusting; the women hawk on the floor; the forks are dirty; the trees are poor; the Pont Neuf is not a patch on London Bridge; the cows are skinny; morals are licentious; polish is good; cabbages cost so much; bread is made of coarse flour; Mr Drumgold could not with patience mention the character of John James Rousseau; the Coles are distantly related to the Herberts; and a French turkey is about the size of an English hen. How natural it all is! How admirable Mr Cole would be at home in his own parish! How gladly we will read sixteen volumes about life in Bletchley if Miss Waddell will print them! But the present volume is nothing short of torture. 'Cole,' one is inclined to cry, 'if you don't give up sightseeing to-day, if you don't dine with Mr Walpole, if you don't report every word he says, leaving Drumgold out of it altogether, if you don't turn the talk somehow upon Madame du Deffand, if you don't somehow tell us more about one of the most curious affairs of the heart that was ever transacted, or failing that, rake up a few odds and ends of interest about that amazing society that was playing spillikins on the verge of revolution, we will –' But what can we do? The dead have no sense whatever of what is due to posterity. Mr Cole imperturbably pulls on his boots and proceeds to visit the Sorbonne.

Must one then read *Guy Mannering*, or take Jane Austen from the bookshelf? No, the advantage of belonging to a good library is that it is only upon very exceptional occasions that one need have recourse to the classics. New books, in fresh jackets, are delivered daily, and good books, too – *Things I Remember*, by the Grand Duchess Marie of Russia, for instance, a very terrible book; *The Diary of a Somersetshire Parson* – a very absorbing book; *By Guess and by God* – a very exciting yet infinitely childish book; and *Scrutinies*, a collection of critical essays by various writers. But what kind of book is *Scrutinies*? That, indeed, I cannot tell you at the moment for the good reason that I have not read it; but you can guess from the title and a glance at the table of contents that it consists of articles by the tolerably young – Messrs Alec Brown, B. Higgins, Mary Butts, Jack Lindsay, P. Quennell, Sherard Vines, C. Saltmarshe, and so on, upon the tolerably old – Messrs Eliot, Huxley, Joyce, Lawrence, Sitwell, Strachey, and so on. And if I hesitate to read beyond the title page at present it is for the very sound and simple reason that it is so much pleasanter to look upon the young than upon the old, the young who are fresh and pliable, who have not stood out in the storm and stiffened into attitudes and hardened into wrinkles. Beauty is theirs now, as soon the future will be theirs also. Let us, therefore, leave the figures of the elders where they stand and turn our bull's eye upon the advancing and victorious hordes of youth.

And what is our first impression as we look? A very strange one. How orderly they come! One could swear that they are all arrayed in troops, and all march in step, and all halt, charge and otherwise behave themselves under the command of officers mounted upon chargers. As far as one can see – a bull's eye, it must be admitted, is not a very steady or comprehensive weapon – there is not a single straggler or deserter among them; there is no dancing or disorder; no wild voice cries alone; no man or woman breaks the ranks and leaves the troop and takes to the wilderness stirring desire and unrest among the hearts of his companions. All is orderly, all is preconcerted. If division there is, even that is regular. Camp is opposed to camp; the hostile parties separate, form, meet, fight, leave each other for dead upon the ground; rise, form and fight again. Classic is opposed to romantic; naturalist to metaphysic.

Never was there such a sight since the world began. Never – as they come nearer this too becomes certain – were the young so well equipped as at present. No more respectable army has ever issued from the portals of the two great Universities – none more courageous, more instructed, more outspoken, more intolerant of humbug in all its forms, better fitted to deal pretence its death and falsity its finish – and yet (for all these flowers, of course, conceal a viper) there is a fatal defect; they do not lead, they follow. Where is the adventurous, the intolerant, the immensely foolish young man or woman who dares to be himself? He or she must, of course, be there. He or she will in time to come make himself known. But at present, since he always keeps the ranks, since if he fights he is careful, like Sir Walter Blunt in *Henry the Fourth*, to wear the armour of his king, there is no knowing him at present from the seven hundred and fifty-five others who are similarly disguised.

If this is true, if there is now a uniformity and a drill and a discretion unknown before, what do you think can be the reason? In one word, and I have room for one only, and that is murmured in your private ear – education. Some years since, for reasons unknown, but presumably of value, it must have occurred to someone that the arts of reading and of writing can be taught. Degrees were given at the Universities to those who showed proficiency in their native tongue. And the teachers of the living language were not old and hoary; as fitted their subject they were young and supple. Persuasion sat on their tongues, and the taught, instead of mocking, loved their teachers. And the teachers took the manuscripts of the young and drew circles of blue chalk round this adjective and circles of red chalk round that adverb. They added in purple ink what Pope would have thought and what Wordsworth would have said. And the young, since they loved their teachers, believed them. Hence it came about that, instead of knowing that the sun was in the sky and the bird on the branch, the young knew the whole course of English literature from one end to another; how one age follows another; and one influence cancels another; and one style is derived from another; and one phrase is better than another. They took service under their teachers instead of riding into battle alone. All their marriages – and what are the five years between twenty and twenty-five in the life of a writer but years of courtship and wedding, of falling in love with words and learning their nature, how to mate them by one's own decree in sentences of one's own framing? – all their marriages were arranged in public; tutors introduced the couples; lecturers supervised the amours; and examiners finally pronounced whether the fruit of the union was blessed or the reverse. Such methods, of course, produce an erudite and eugenic offspring. But, one asks, turning over the honest, the admirable, the entirely sensible and unsentimental pages, where is love? Meaning by that, where is the sound of the sea and the red of the rose; where is music, imagery, and a voice speaking from the heart?

That this is all great nonsense I am well aware. But what else can you expect in a letter? The time has come to open *Scrutinies* and begin to read – no, the time has come to rake out the cinders and go to bed.

The Rev. William Cole: A Letter

My Dear William,

In my opinion you are keeping something back. Last year when you went to Paris and did not see Madame du Deffand but measured the exact length of every nose on every tombstone – I can assure you they have grown no longer or shorter since – I was annoyed, I admit. But I had the sense to see that, after all, you were alive, and a clergyman, and from Bletchley – in fact, you were as much out of place in Paris as a cowslip impaled upon the diamond horns of a duchess's tiara. Put him back in Bletchley, I said, plant him in his own soil, let him burble on in his own fashion, and the miracle will happen. The cows will low; the church bells will ring; all Bletchley will come alive; and, reading over William's shoulder, we shall see deep, deep into the hearts of Mrs Willis and Mr Robinson.

I regret to tell you that I was wrong. You are not a cowslip. You do not bloom. The hearts of Mrs Willis and Mr Robinson remain sealed books to us. You write Jan. 16th, 1766, and it is precisely as if I had written Jan. 16th, 1932. In other words, you have rubbed all the bloom off two hundred years and that is so rare a feat – it implies something so queer in the writer – that I am intrigued and puzzled and cannot help asking you to enlighten me. Are you simply a bore, William? No, that is out of the question.

In the first place, Horace Walpole did not tolerate bores, or write to them, or go for country jaunts with them; in the second, Miss Waddell loves you. You shed all round you, in the eyes of Miss Waddell, that mysterious charm which those we love impart to their meanest belongings. She loves your parrot; she commiserates your cat. Every room in your house is familiar to her. She knows about your Gothic chamber and your neat arched bed; she knows how many steps led up to the pantry and down to the summer house; she knows, she approves, how you spent every hour of your day. She sees the neighbours through the light of your eyes. She laughs at some; she likes others; she knows who was fat and who was thin, and who told lies, who had a bad leg, and who was no better than she should have been. Mr and Mrs Barton, Thomas Tansley, Mr and Mrs Lord of Mursley, the Diceys, and Dr Pettingal, are all real and alive to her; so are your roses, your horses, your nectarines and your knats.

Would that I could see through her eyes! Alas, wherever I look I see blight and mildew. The moss never grows upon your walls. Your nectarines never ripen. The blackbird sings, but out of tune. The knats — and you say 'I hardly know a place so pestered with that vermin as Bletchley' — bite, just like our gnats. As for the human beings they pass through the same disenchantment. Not that I have any fault to find with your friends or with Bletchley either. Nobody is very good, but then nobody is very bad. Tom sometimes hits a hare, oftener he misses, the fish sometimes bite, but not always; if it freezes it also thaws, and though the harvest was not bad it might have been better. But now, William, confess. We know in our hearts, you and I, that England in the eighteenth century was not like this. We know from Woodforde, from Walpole, from Thomas Turner, from

Skinner, from Gray, from Fielding, from Jane Austen, from
scores of memoirs and letters, from a thousand forgotten
stone masons, bricklayers and cabinet makers, from a myriad
sources, that I have not learning to name or space to quote,
that England was a substantial, beautiful country in the
eighteenth century; aristocratic and common; hand-made
and horse-ploughed; an eating, drinking, bastard-begetting,
laughing, cursing, humorous, eccentric, lovable land. If with
your pen in your hand and the date facing you, Jan. 16th,
1766, you see none of all this, then the fault is yours. Some
spite has drawn a veil across your eyes. Indeed, there are
pouches under them I could swear. You slouch as you
walk. You switch at thistles half-heartedly with your stick.
You do not much enjoy your food. Gossip has no relish
for you. You mention the 'scandalous story of Mr Felton
Hervey, his two daughters and a favourite footman' and
add, 'I hope it is not true.' So do I, but I cannot put much
life into my hoping when you withhold the facts. You stop
Pettingal in the middle of his boasting – you cut him short
with a sarcasm – just as he was proving that the Greeks
liked toasted cheese and was deriving the word Bergamy
from the Arabic. As for Madame Geoffrin, you never lose
a chance of saying something disobliging about that lady;
a coffee-pot has only to be reputed French for you to
defame it. Then look how touchy you are – you grumble,
the servants are late with the papers, you complain, Mr Pitt
never thanked you for the pigeons (yet Horace Walpole
thought you a philosopher); then how you suspect people's
motives; how you bid fathers thresh their little boys; how
you are sure the servant steals the onions. All these are
marks of a thin-blooded poverty-stricken disposition. And
yet – you are a good man; you visit the poor; you bury
the infected; you have been educated at Cambridge; you

venerate antiquity. The truth is that you are concealing something, even from Miss Waddell.

Why, I ask, did you write this diary and lock it in a chest with iron hoops and insist that no one was to read it or publish it for twenty years after your death unless it were that you had something on your mind, something that you wished to confess and get rid of? You are not one of those people who love life so well that they cherish even the memory of roast mutton, like Woodforde; you did not hate life so much that you must shriek out your curse on it, like poor Skinner. You write and write, ramblingly, list-lessly, like a person who is trying to bring himself to say the thing that will explain to himself what is wrong with himself. And you find it very hard. You would rather mention anything but that – Miss Chester, I mean, and the boat on the Avon. You cannot force yourself to admit that you have kept that lock of hair in your drawer these thirty years. When Mrs Robinson, her daughter, asked you for it (March 19th, 1766) you said you could not find it. But you were not easy under that concealment. You did at length go to your private drawer (Nov. 26th, 1766) and there it was, as you well knew. But even so, with the lock of hair in your hand, you still seek to put us off the scent. You ramble on about giving Mrs Robinson a barrel of oysters; about potted rabbits; about the weather, until suddenly out it comes, 'Gave Mrs Robinson a braided Lock of Lady Robinson's Mother's hair (and Sister to Mrs Robinson of Cransley), which I cut off in a Boat on the River Avon at Bath about 30 years ago when my Sister Jane and myself were much acquainted with her, then Miss Chester.' There we have it. The poisoned tooth is out. You were once young and ardent and very much in love. Passion overcame you. You were alone. The wind blew a lock of Miss Chester's hair from beneath her hat. You reached forward. You cut it. And then? Nothing. That is your tragedy – you yourself failed yourself. You think of that scene twenty times a day, I believe, as you saunter, rather heavily, along the damp paths at Bletchley. That is the dreary little tune that you hum as you stoop over your parments measuring noses, deciphering dates – 'I failed, failed, failed on the boat on the Avon.' That is why your nectarines are blighted; and the parrot dies; and the parlour cat is scalded; and you love nobody except, perhaps, your little dun-coloured horse. That is why you 'always had a mind to live retired in Glamorganshire.' That is why Mr Pitt never thanked you for the pigeons. That is why Mr Stonehewer became His Majesty's Historiographer, while you visited paupers in Fenny Stratford. That is why he never came to see you, and why you observed so bitterly, that 'people suffer themselves to forget their old friends when they are surrounded by the great and are got above the world.' You see, William, if you hoard a failure, if you come to grudge even the sun for shining – and that, I think, is what you did – fruit does not ripen; a blight falls upon parrots and cats; people would actually rather that you did not give them pigeons.

But enough. I may be wrong. Miss Chester's hair may have nothing to do with it. And Miss Waddell may be right – every good quality of heart and head may be yours. I am sure I hope so. But I beg, William, now that you are about to begin a fresh volume, at Cambridge too, with men of character and learning, that you will pull yourself together. Speak out. Justify the faith that Miss Waddell has in you. For you are keeping one of the finest scholars of her time shut up in the British Museum among mummies and policemen and wet umbrellas. There must be a trifle of ninety-five volumes more of you in those iron-bound chests. Lighten her task; relieve our anxiety, and so add to the gratitude of your obliged obedient servant,

Virginia Woolf.

Archbishop Thomson

The origin of Archbishop Thomson was obscure. His great-uncle 'may reasonably be supposed' to have been 'an ornament to the middle classes'. His aunt married a gentleman who was present at the murder of Gustavus III of Sweden; and his father met his death at the age of eighty-seven by treading on a cat in the early hours of the morning. The physical vigour which this anecdote implies was combined in the Archbishop with powers of intellect which promised success in whatever profession he adopted. At Oxford it seemed likely that he would devote himself to philosophy or science. While reading for his degree he found time to write the *Outlines of the Laws of Thought*, which 'immediately became a recognised text-book for Oxford classes'. But though poetry, philosophy, medicine, and the law held out their temptations he put such thoughts aside, or never entertained them, having made up his mind from the first to dedicate himself to Divine service. The measure of his success in the more exalted sphere is attested by the following facts: Ordained deacon in 1842 at the age of twenty-three, he became Dean and Bursar of Queen's College, Oxford, in 1845; Provost in 1855, Bishop of Gloucester and Bristol in 1861, and Archbishop of York in 1862. Thus at the early age of forty-three he stood next in rank to the Archbishop of Canterbury himself; and it was commonly though erroneously expected that he would in the end attain to that dignity also.

It is a matter of temperament and belief whether you read this list with respect or with boredom; whether you look upon an archbishop's hat as a crown or as an extinguisher. If, like the present reviewer, you are ready to hold the simple faith that the outer order corresponds to the inner – that a vicar is a good man, a canon a better man, and an archbishop the best man of all – you will find the study of the Archbishop's life one of extreme fascination. He has turned aside from poetry and philosophy and law, and specialised in virtue. He has dedicated himself to the service of the Divine. His spiritual proficiency has been such that he has developed from deacon to dean, from dean to bishop, and from bishop to archbishop in the short space of twenty years. As there are only two archbishops in the whole of England the inference seems to be that he is the second best man in England; his hat is the proof of it. Even in a material sense his hat was one of the largest; it was larger than Mr Gladstone's; larger than Thackeray's; larger than Dickens's; it was in fact, so his hatter told him and we are inclined to agree, an 'eight full'. Yet he began much as other men begin. He struck an undergraduate in a fit of temper and was rusticated; he wrote a text-book of logic and rowed a very good oar. But after he was ordained his diary shows that the specialising process had begun. He thought a great deal about the state of the soul; about 'the monstrous tumour of Simony'; about Church reform; and about the meaning of Christianity. 'Self-renunciation,' he came to the conclusion, 'is the foundation of Christian Religion and Christian Morals . . . The highest wisdom is that which can enforce and cultivate this self-renunciation. Hence (against Cousin) I hold that religion is higher far than philosophy. There is one mention of chemists and capillarity, but science and philosophy were, even at this early stage, in danger of being crowded out. Soon the diary takes a different tone. 'He seems,' says his biographer, 'to have had no time for committing his thoughts to paper'; he records his engagements only, and he dines out almost every night. Sir Henry Taylor, whom he met at one of these parties, described him as 'simple, solid, good, capable, and pleasing'. Perhaps it was his solidity combined with his 'eminently scientific' turn of mind, his blandness as well as his bulk, that impressed some of these great people with the confidence that in him the Church had found a very necessary champion. His 'brawny logic' and massive frame seemed to fit him to grapple with a task that taxed the strongest – how, that is, to reconcile the scientific discoveries of the age with religion, and even prove them 'some of the strongest witnesses for the truth'. If any one could do this Thomson could; his practical ability, unhampered by any mystical or dreaming tendency, had already proved itself in the conduct of the business affairs of his College. From Bishop he became almost instantly Archbishop; and in becoming Archbishop he became Primate of England, Governor of the Charterhouse and King's College, London, patron of one hundred and twenty livings, with the Archdeaconries of York, Cleveland, and the East Riding in his gift, and the Canonries and Prebends in York Minster. Bishopthorpe itself was an enormous palace; he was immediately faced by the 'knotty question' of whether to buy all the furniture – 'much of it only poor stuff' – or to furnish the house anew, which would cost a fortune. Moreover there were seven cows in the park; but these, perhaps, were counterbalanced by nine children in the nursery. Then the Prince and Princess of Wales came to stay, and the Archbishop took upon himself the task of furnishing the Princess's apartments. He went up to London and bought eight Moderator lamps, two Spanish figures holding candles, and reminded himself of the necessity of buying 'soap for Princess'. But meanwhile far more serious matters claimed every ounce of his strength. Already he had been exhorted to 'wield the sure lance of your brawny logic against the sophistries' of the authors of *Essays and Reviews*, and had responded in a work called *Aids to Faith*. Near at hand the town of Sheffield, with its large population of imperfectly educated working men, was a breeding ground of scepticism and discontent. The Archbishop made it his special charge. He was fond of watching the rolling of armour plate, and constantly addressed meetings of working men. 'Now what are these Nihilisms, and Socialisms, and Communisms, and Fenianisms, and Secret Societies – what do they all mean?' he asked. 'Selfishness,' he replied, and 'assertion of one class against the rest is at the bottom of them all'. There was a law of nature, he said, by which wages went up and wages went down. 'You must accept the declivity as well as the ascent . . . If we could only get people to learn that, then things would go on a great deal better and smoother.' And the working men of Sheffield responded by giving him five hundred pieces of cutlery mounted in sterling silver. But presumably there were a certain number of knives among the spoons and the forks.

Bishop Colenso, however, was far more troublesome than the working men of Sheffield; and the Ritualists vexed him so persistently that even his vast strength felt the strain. The questions which were referred to him for decision were peculiarly fitted to tease and annoy even a man of his bulk and his blandness. Shall a drunkard found dead in a ditch, or a burglar who has fallen through a skylight, be given the benefit of the Burial Service? he was asked. The question of lighted candles was 'most difficult'; the wearing of coloured stoles and the administration of the mixed chalice taxed him considerably; and finally there was the Rev. John Purchas, who, dressed in cope, alb, biretta and stole 'cross-wise', lit candles and extinguished them 'for no special reason'; filled a vessel with black powder and rubbed it into the foreheads of his congregation; and hung over the Holy Table 'a figure, image, or stuffed skin of a dove, in a flying attitude'. The Archbishop's temper, usually so positive and imperturbable, was gravely ruffled, 'Will there ever come a time when it will be thought a crime to have striven to keep the Church of England as representing the common sense of the Nation? he asked. 'I suppose it may, but I shall not see it. I have gone through a good deal, but I do not repent of having done my best.' If, for a moment, the Archbishop himself could ask such a question, we must confess to a state of complete bewilderment. What has become of our superlatively good man? He is harassed and cumbered; spends his time settling questions about stuffed pigeons and coloured petticoats; writes over eighty letters before breakfast sometimes; scarcely has time to run over to Paris and buy his daughter a bonnet; and in the end has to ask himself whether one of these days his conduct will not be considered a crime.

Was it a crime? And if so, was it his fault? Did he not start out in the belief that Christianity had something to do with renunciation and was not entirely a matter of common sense? If honours and obligations, pomps and possessions, accumulated and encrusted him, how, being an Archbishop, could he refuse to accept them? Princesses must have their soap; palaces must have their furniture; children must have their cows. And, pathetic though it seems, he never completely lost his interest in science. He wore a pedometer; he was one of the first to use a camera; he believed in the future of the typewriter; and in his last years he tried to mend a broken clock. He was a delightful father too; he wrote witty, terse, sensible letters; his good stories were much to the point; and he died in harness. Certainly he was a very able man, but if we insist upon goodness – is it easy, is it possible, for a good man to be an Archbishop?

Miss Ormerod

The trees stood massively in all their summer foliage spotted and grouped upon a meadow which sloped gently down from the big white house. There were unmistakable signs of the year 1835 both in the trees and in the sky, for modern trees are not nearly so voluminous as these ones, and the sky of those days had a kind of pale diffusion in its texture which was different from the more concentrated tone of the skies we know.

Mr George Ormerod stepped from the drawing-room window of Sedbury House, Gloucestershire, wearing a tall furry hat and white trousers strapped under his instep; he was closely, though deferentially, followed by a lady wearing a yellow-spotted dress over a crinoline, and behind her, singly and arm in arm, came nine children in nankeen jackets and long white drawers. They were going to see the water let out of a pond.

The youngest child, Eleanor, a little girl with a pale face, rather elongated features, and black hair, was left by herself in the drawing-room, a large sallow apartment with pillars, two chandeliers for some reason enclosed in Holland bags, and several octagonal tables, some of inlaid wood and others of greenish malachite. At one of these little Eleanor Ormerod was seated in a high chair.

'Now Eleanor,' said her mother, as the party assembled

for the expedition to the pond, 'here are some pretty beetles. Don't touch the glass. Don't get down from your chair, and when we come back little George will tell you all about it.'

So saying, Mrs Ormerod placed a tumbler of water containing about half a dozen great water grubs in the middle of the malachite table, at a safe distance from the child, and followed her husband down the slope of old-fashioned turf towards a cluster of extremely old-fashioned sheep; opening, directly she stepped on to the terrace, a tiny parasol of bottle green silk with a bottle green fringe, though the sky was like nothing so much as a flock bed covered with a counterpane of white dimity.

The plump pale grubs gyrated slowly round and round in the tumbler. So simple an entertainment must surely soon have ceased to satisfy. Surely Eleanor would shake the tumbler, upset the grubs, and scramble down from her chair. Why, even a grown person can hardly watch those grubs crawling down the glass wall, then floating to the surface, without a sense of boredom not untinged with disgust. But the child sat perfectly still. Was it her custom, then, to be entertained by the gyrations of grubs? Her eyes were reflective, even critical. But they shone with increasing excitement. She beat one hand upon the edge of the table. What was the reason? One of the grubs had ceased to float: he lay at the bottom; the rest, descending, proceeded to tear him to pieces.

'And how has little Eleanor enjoyed herself?' asked Mr Ormerod, in rather a deep voice, stepping into the room and with a slight air of heat and of fatigue upon his face.

'Papa,' said Eleanor almost interrupting her father in her eagerness to impart her observations, 'I saw one of the grubs fall down and the rest came and ate him!'

'Nonsense, Eleanor,' said Mr Ormerod. 'You are not telling the truth.' He looked severely at the tumbler in which the beetles were still gyrating as before.

'Papa, it was true!'

'Eleanor, little girls are not allowed to contradict their fathers,' said Mrs Ormerod, coming in through the window, and closing her green parasol with a snap.

'Let this be a lesson,' Mr Ormerod began, signing to the other children to approach, when the door opened, and the servant announced,

'Captain Fenton.'

Captain Fenton 'was at times thought to be tedious in his recurrence to the charge of the Scots Greys in which he had served at the battle of Waterloo'.

But what is this crowd gathered round the door of the George Hotel in Chepstow? A faint cheer rises from the bottom of the hill. Up comes the mail coach, horses steaming, panels mud-splashed. 'Make way! Make way!' cries the ostler and the vehicle dashed into the courtyard, pulls up sharp before the door. Down jumps the coachman, the horses are led off, and a fine team of spanking greys is harnessed with incredible speed in their stead. Upon all this – coachman, horses, coach, and passengers – the crowd looked with gaping admiration every Wednesday evening all through the year. But today, the twelfth of March, 1852, as the coachman settled his rug, and stretched his hands for the reins, he observed that instead of being fixed upon him, the eyes of the people of Chepstow darted this way and that. Heads were jerked. Arms flung out. Here a hat swooped in a semi-circle. Off drove the coach almost unnoticed. As it turned the corner all the outside passengers craned their necks, and one gentleman rose to his feet and shouted,

'There! there! there!' before he was bowled into eternity. It was an insect – a red-winged insect. Out the people of Chepstow poured into the high road; down the hill they ran; always the insect flew in front of them; at length by Chepstow Bridge a young man, throwing his bandanna over the blade of an oar, captured it alive and presented it to a highly respectable elderly gentleman who now came puffing upon the scene – Samuel Budge, doctor, of Chepstow. By Samuel Budge it was presented to Miss Ormerod; by her sent to a professor at Oxford. And he, declaring it 'a fine specimen of the rose under-winged locust' added the gratifying information that it 'was the first of the kind to be captured so far west'.

And so, at the age of twenty-four Miss Eleanor Ormerod was thought the proper person to receive the gift of a locust.

When Eleanor Ormerod appeared at archery meetings and croquet tournaments young men pulled their whiskers and young ladies looked grave. It was so difficult to make friends with a girl who could talk of nothing but black beetles and earwigs – 'Yes, that's what she likes, isn't it queer? – Why, the other day Ellen, Mama's maid, heard from Jane, who's under-kitchenmaid at Sedbury House, that Eleanor tried to boil a beetle in the kitchen saucepan and he wouldn't die, and swam round and round, and she got into a terrible state and sent the groom all the way to Gloucester to fetch chloroform – all for an insect my dear! – and she gives the cottagers shillings to collect beetles for her – and she spends hours in her bedroom cutting them up – and she climbs trees like a boy to find wasps' nests – oh, you can't think what they don't say about her in the village – for she does look so odd, dressed anyhow, with that great big nose and those bright little eyes, so like a caterpillar herself, I always think — but of course she's wonderfully clever and very good, too, both of them. Georgiana has a lending library for the cottagers, and Eleanor never misses a service — but there she is — that short pale girl in the large bonnet. Do go and talk to her, for I'm sure I'm too stupid, but you'd find plenty to say —' But neither Fred nor Arthur, Henry nor William found anything to say —

'. . . probably the lecturer would have been equally well pleased had none of her own sex put in an appearance.'

This comment upon a lecture delivered in the year 1889 throws some light, perhaps, upon archery meetings in the 'fifties.

It being nine o'clock on a February night some time about 1862 all the Ormerods were in the library; Mr Ormerod making architectural designs at a table; Mrs Ormerod lying on a sofa making pencil drawings upon grey paper; Eleanor making a model of a snake to serve as a paper weight; Georgiana making a copy of the font in Tidenham Church; some of the others examining books with beautiful illustrations; while at intervals someone rose, unlocked the wire book case, took down a volume for instruction or entertainment, and perused it beneath the chandelier.

Mr Ormerod required complete silence for his studies. His word was law, even to the dogs, who, in the absence of their master, instinctively obeyed the eldest male person in the room. Some whispered colloquy there might be between Mrs Ormerod and her daughters —

'The draught under the pew was really worse than ever this morning, Mama —'

'And we could only unfasten the latch in the chancel

because Eleanor happened to have her ruler with her –'

'– hm – m – m. Dr Armstrong – Hm – m – m –'

'– Anyhow things aren't as bad with us as they are at Kinghampton. They say Mrs Briscoe's Newfoundland dog follows her right up to the chancel rails when she takes the sacrament – '

'And the turkey is still sitting on its eggs in the pulpit.'

– 'The period of incubation for a turkey is between three and four weeks' – said Eleanor thoughtfully looking up from her cast of the snake and forgetting, in the interest of her subject, to speak in a whisper.

'Am I to be allowed no peace in my own house?' Mr Ormerod exclaimed angrily, rapping with his ruler on the table, upon which Mrs Ormerod half shut one eye and squeezed a little blob of Chinese white on to her high light, and they remained silent until the servants came in, when everyone, with the exception of Mrs Ormerod, fell on their knees. For she, poor lady, suffered from a chronic complaint and left the family party for ever a year or two later, when the green sofa was moved into the corner, and the drawings given to her nieces in memory of her. But Mr Ormerod went on making architectural drawings at nine p.m. every night (save on Sundays when he read a sermon) until he too lay upon the green sofa, which had not been used since Mrs Ormerod lay there, but still looked much the same. 'We deeply felt the happiness of ministering to his welfare,' Miss Ormerod wrote, 'for he would not hear of our leaving him for even twenty-four hours and he objected to visits from my brothers excepting occasionally for a short time. They, not being used to the gentle ways necessary for an aged invalid, worried him . . . the Thursday following, the 9th October, 1873, he passed gently away at the mature age of eighty-seven years.' Oh, graves in country churchyards

– respectable burials – mature old gentlemen – D.C.L., L.L.D., F.R.S., F.S.A. – lots of letters comes after your names, but lots of women are buried with you!

There remained the Hessian Fly and the Bot – mysterious insects! Not, one would have thought, among God's most triumphant creations, and yet – if you see them under a microscope! – the Bot, obese, globular, obscene; the Hessian, booted, spurred, whiskered, cadaverous. Next slip under the glass an innocent grain; behold it pock-marked and livid; or take this strip of hide, and note those odious pullulating lumps – well, what does the landscape look like then?

The only palatable object for the eye to rest on in acres of England is a lump of Paris Green. But English people won't use microscopes; you can't make them use Paris Green either – or if they do, they let it drip. Dr Ritzema Bos is a great stand-by. For they won't take a woman's word. And indeed, though for the sake of the Ox Warble one must stretch a point, there are matters, questions of stock infestation, things one has to go into – things a lady doesn't even like to see, much less discuss in print – 'these, I say, I intend to leave entirely to the Veterinary surgeons. My brother – oh, he's dead now – a very good man – for whom I collected wasps' nests – lived at Brighton and wrote about wasps – he, I say, wouldn't let me learn anatomy, never liked me to do more than take sections of teeth.'

Ah, but Eleanor, the Bot and the Hessian have more power over you than Mr Edward Ormerod himself. Under the microscope you clearly perceive that these insects have organs, orifices, excrement; they do, most emphatically, copulate. Escorted on the one side by the Bot or Warble, on the other by the Hessian Fly, Miss Ormerod advanced statelily, if slowly, into the open. Never did her features show more sublime than when lit up by the candour of her avowal. 'This is excrement; these, though Ritzema Bos is positive to the contrary, are the generative organs of the male. I've proved it.' Upon her head the hood of Edinburgh most fitly descended; pioneer of purity even more than of Paris Green.

'If you're sure I'm not in your way,' said Miss Lipscomb unstrapping her paint box and planting her tripod firmly on the path, '– I'll try to get a picture of those lovely hydrangeas against the sky – What flowers you have in Penzance!'

The market gardener crossed his hands on his hoe, slowly twined a piece of bass round his finger, looked at the sky, said something about the sun, also about the prevalence of lady artists, and then, with a nod of his head, observed sententiously that it was to a lady that he owed everything he had.

'Ah?' said Miss Lipscomb, flattered, but already much occupied with her composition.

'A lady with a queer sounding name,' said Mr Pascoe, 'but that's the lady I've called my little girl after – I don't think there's such another in Christendom.'

Of course it was Miss Ormerod, equally of course Miss Lipscomb was the sister of Miss Ormerod's family doctor; and so she did no sketching that morning, but left with a handsome bunch of grapes instead – for every flower had drooped, ruin had stared him in the face – he had written, not believing one bit what they told him – to the lady with the queer name, back there came a book 'In-ju-ri-ous In-sects,' with the page turned down, perhaps by her very hand, also a letter which he kept at home under the clock, but he knew every word by heart, since it was due to what she said there that he wasn't a ruined man – and tears ran down his face and Miss Lipscomb, clearing a space on the lodging-house table, wrote the whole story to her brother.

'The prejudice against Paris Green certainly seems to be dying down,' said Miss Ormerod when she read it. – 'But now,' she sighed rather heavily being no longer young and much afflicted with the gout, 'now it's the sparrows.'

One might have thought that *they* would have left her alone – innocent dirt-grey birds, taking more than their share of the breakfast crumbs, otherwise inoffensive. But once you look through a microscope – once you see the Hessian and the Bot as they really are – there's no peace for an elderly lady pacing her terrace on a fine May morning. For example, why, when there are crumbs enough for all, do only the sparrows get them? Why not swallows or martins? Why – oh, here come the servants for prayers –

'Forgive us our trepasses as we forgive them that trespass against us . . . For thine is the Kingdom and the power and the glory, for ever and ever. Amen –'

'*The Times* ma'am –'

'Thank you, Dixon . . . The Queen's birthday! We must drink her Majesty's health in the old white port, Dixon. Home Rule – tut – tut – tut. All that madman Gladstone. My father would have thought the world was coming to an end, and I'm not at all sure that it isn't. I must talk to Dr Lipscombe –'

Yet all the time in the tail of her eye she saw myriads of sparrows, and retiring to the study proclaimed in a pamphlet of which 36,000 copies were gratuitously distributed that the sparrow is a pest.

'When he eats an insect,' she said to her sister Georgiana, 'which isn't often, it's one of the few insects that one wants to keep – one of the very few,' she added with a touch of acidity natural to one whose investigations have all tended to the discredit of the insect race.

'But there'll be some very unpleasant consequence to face,' she concluded – 'Very unpleasant indeed.'

Happily the port was now brought in, the servants assembled; and Miss Ormerod, rising to her feet, gave the toast 'Her Blessed Majesty.' She was extremely loyal, and moreover she liked nothing better than a glass of her father's old white port. She kept his pigtail, too, in a box.

Such being her disposition it went hard with her to analyse the sparrow's crop, for the sparrow she felt, symbolises something of the homely virtue of English domestic life, and to proclaim it stuffed with deceit was disloyal to much that she, and her fathers before her, held dear. Sure enough the clergy – the Rev. J. E. Walker – denounced her for her brutality; 'God Save the Sparrow!' exclaimed the Animal's Friend; and Miss Carrington, of the Humanitarian League, replied in a leaflet described by Miss Ormerod as 'spirity, discourteous, and inaccurate.

'Well,' said Miss Ormerod to her sister, 'it did me no harm before to be threatened to be shot at, also hanged in effigy, and other little attentions.'

'Still it was very disagreeable, Eleanor – more disagreeable I believe, to me than to you,' said Georgiana. Soon Georgiana died. She had however finished the beautiful series of insect diagrams at which she worked every morning in the dining-room and they were presented to Edinburgh University. But Eleanor was never the same woman after that.

Dear forest fly – flour moths – weevils – grouse and cheese flies – beetles – foreign correspondents – eel worms – ladybirds – wheat midges – resignation from the Royal Agricultural Society – gall mites – boot beetles

– Announcement of honorary degree to be conferred – feelings of appreciation and anxiety – paper on wasps – last annual report – warnings of serious illness – proposed pension – gradual loss of strength – Finally Death.

That is life, so they say.

'It does no good to keep people waiting for an answer,' sighed Miss Ormerod, 'though I don't feel as able as I did since that unlucky accident at Waterloo. And no one realises what the strain of the work is – often I'm the only lady in the room, and the gentlemen so learned, though I've always found them most helpful, most generous in every way. But I'm growing old, Miss Hartwell, that's what it is. That's what led me to be thinking of this difficult matter of flour infestation in the middle of the road so that I didn't see the horse until he had poked his nose into my ear . . . Then there's this nonsense about a pension. What could possess Mr Barron to think of such a thing? I should feel inexpressibly lowered if I accepted a pension. Why, I don't altogether like writing LL.D. after my name, though Georgie would have liked it. All I ask is to be let go on in my own quiet way. Now where is Messrs Langridge's sample? We must take that first. "Gentlemen, I have examined your sample and find . . ."'

'If any one deserves a thorough good rest it's you, Miss Ormerod,' said Dr Lipscomb, who had grown a little white over the ears. 'I should say the farmers of England ought to set up a statue to you, bring offerings of corn and wine – make you a kind of Goddess, eh – what was her name?'

'Not a very shapely figure for a Goddess,' said Miss Ormerod with a little laugh. 'I should enjoy the wine though. You're not going to cut me off my one glass of port surely?'

'You must remember,' said Dr Lipscomb, shaking his head, 'how much your life means to others.'

'Well, I don't know about that,' said Miss Ormerod, pondering a little. 'To be sure, I've chosen my epitaph. "She introduced Paris Green into England," and there might be a word or two about the Hessian fly – that, I do believe, was a good piece of work.'

'No need to think about epitaphs yet,' said Dr Lipscomb.

'Our lives are in the hands of the Lord,' said Miss Ormerod simply.

Dr Lipscomb bent his head and looked out of the window. Miss Ormerod remained silent.

'English entomologists care little or nothing for objects of practical importance,' she exclaimed suddenly. 'Take this question of flour infestation – I can't say how many grey hairs that hasn't grown me.'

'Figuratively speaking, Miss Ormerod,' said Dr Lipscomb, for her hair was still raven black.

'Well, I do believe all good work is done in concert,' Miss Ormerod continued. 'It is often a great comfort to me to think that.'

'It's beginning to rain,' said Dr Lipscomb. 'How will your enemies like that, Miss Ormerod?'

'Hot or cold, wet or dry, insects always flourish!' cried Miss Ormerod energetically sitting up in bed.

'Old Miss Ormerod is dead,' said Mr Drummond, opening *The Times* on Saturday, July 20th, 1901.

'Old Miss Ormerod?' asked Mrs Drummond.

Education

Two Women

Up to the beginning of the nineteenth century the distinguished woman had almost invariably been an aristocrat. It was the great lady who ruled and wrote letters and influenced the course of politics. From the huge middle class few women rose to eminence, nor has the drabness of their lot received the attention which has been bestowed upon the splendours of the great and the miseries of the poor. There they remain, even in the early part of the nineteenth century, a vast body, living, marrying, bearing children in dull obscurity until at last we begin to wonder whether there was something in their condition itself – in the age at which they married, the number of children they bore, the privacy they lacked, the incomes they had not, the conventions which stifled them, and the education they never received which so affected them that though the middle class is the great reservoir from which we draw our distinguished men it has thrown up singularly few women to set beside them.

The profound interest of Lady Stephen's life of Miss Emily Davies lies in the light it throws upon this dark and obscure chapter of human history. Miss Davies was born in the year 1830, of middle-class parents who could afford to educate their sons but not their daughters. Her education was, she supposed, much the same as that of other clergymen's daughters at that time. 'Do they go to school?

No. Do they have governesses at home? No. They have lessons and get on as they can.' But if their positive education had stopped at a little Latin, a little history, a little housework, it would not so much have mattered. It was what may be called the negative education, that which decrees not what you may do but what you may not do, that cramped and stifled. 'Probably only women who have laboured under it can understand the weight of discouragement produced by being perpetually told that, as women, nothing much is ever expected of them . . . Women who have lived in the atmosphere produced by such teaching know how it stifles and chills; how hard it is to work courageously through it.' Preachers and rulers of both sexes nevertheless formulated the creed and enforced it vigorously. Charlotte Yonge wrote: 'I have no hesitation in declaring my full belief in the inferiority of woman, nor that she brought it upon herself.' She reminded her sex of a painful incident with a snake in the garden which had settled their destiny, Miss Yonge said, for ever. The mention of Women's Rights made Queen Victoria so furious that 'she cannot contain herself'. Mr Greg, underlining his words, wrote that 'the essentials of a woman's being are *that they are supported by, and they minister to, men*'. The only other occupation allowed them, indeed, was to become a governess or a needlewoman, 'and both these employments were naturally overstocked'. If women wanted to paint there was, up to the year 1858, only one life class in London where they could learn. If they were musical there was the inevitable piano, but the chief aim was to produce a brilliant mechanical execution, and Trollope's picture of four girls all in the same room playing on four pianos all of them out of tune seems to have been, as Trollope's pictures usually are, based on fact. Writing was the most accessible of the arts, and write they did, but their books were deeply influenced by the angle from which they were forced to observe the world. Half-occupied, always interrupted, with much leisure but little time to themselves and no money of their own, these armies of listless women were either driven to find solace and occupation in religion, or, if that failed, they took, as Miss Nightingale said, 'to that perpetual day dreaming which is so dangerous'. Some indeed envied the working classes, and Miss Martineau frankly hailed the ruin of her family with delight. 'I, who had been obliged to write before breakfast, or in some private way, had henceforth liberty to do my own work in my own way, for we had lost our gentility.' But the time had come when there were occasional exceptions both among parents and among daughters. Mr Leigh Smith, for example, allowed his daughter Barbara the same income that he gave his sons. She at once started a school of an advanced character. Miss Garrett became a doctor because her parents, though shocked and anxious, would be reconciled if she were a success. Miss Davies had a brother who sympathised and helped her in her determination to reform the education of women. With such encouragement the three young women started in the middle of the nineteenth century to lead the army of the unemployed in search of work. But the war of one sex upon the rights and possessions of the other is by no means a straightforward affair of attack and victory or defeat. Neither the means nor the end itself is clear-cut and recognised. There is the very potent weapon, for example, of feminine charm – what use were they to make of that? Miss Garrett said she felt 'so mean in trying to come over the doctors by all kinds of little feminine dodges'. Miss Gurney admitted the difficulty, but pointed out that 'Miss Marsh's success among the navvies' had been mainly won by these means, which, for good or for bad, were certainly of immense weight. It was agreed therefore that charm was to be employed. Thus we have the curious spectacle, at once so diverting and so humiliating, of grave and busy women doing fancy work and playing croquet in order that the male eye might be gratified and deceived. 'Three lovely girls' were placed conspicuously in the front row at a meeting, and Miss Garrett herself sat there looking 'exactly like one of the girls whose instinct it is to do what you tell them'. For the arguments that they had to meet by their devious means were in themselves extremely indefinite. There was a thing called 'the tender home-bloom of maidenliness' which must not be touched. There was chastity, of course, and her handmaidens innocence, sweetness, unselfishness, sympathy; all of which might suffer if women were allowed to learn Latin and Greek. The *Saturday Review* gave cogent expression to what men feared for women and needed of women in the year 1864. The idea of submitting young ladies to local university examinations 'almost takes one's breath away', the writer said. If examined they must be, steps must be taken to see that 'learned men advanced in years' were the examiners, and that the presumably aged wives of these aged gentlemen should occupy 'a commanding position in the gallery'. Even so it would be 'next to impossible to persuade the world that a pretty first-class woman came by her honours fairly'. For the truth was, the reviewer wrote, that 'there is a strong and ineradicable male instinct that a learned, or even an accomplished young woman is the most intolerable monster in creation'. It was against instincts and prejudices such as these, tough as roots but intangible as sea mist, that Miss Davies had to fight. Her days passed in a round of the most diverse occupations. Besides the actual labour of raising money and fighting prejudice she had to decide the most delicate moral questions which, directly victory was within sight, began to be posed by the students and their parents. A mother, for example, would only entrust her with her daughter's education on condition that she should come home 'as if nothing had happened', and not 'take to anything eccentric'. The students, on the other hand, bored with watching the Edinburgh express slip a carriage at Hitchin or rolling the lawn with a heavy iron roller, took to playing football, and then invited their teachers to see them act scenes from Shakespeare and Swinburne dressed in men's clothes. This, indeed, was a very serious matter; the great George Eliot was consulted; Mr Russell Gurney was consulted, and also Mr Tomkinson. They decided that it was unwomanly; Hamlet must be played in a skirt.

Miss Davies herself was decidedly austere. When money for the college flowed in she refused to spend it on luxuries. She wanted rooms – always more and more rooms to house those unhappy girls dreaming their youth away in indolence or picking up a little knowledge in the family sitting-room. 'Privacy was the one luxury Miss Davies desired for the student, and in her eyes it was not a luxury – she despised luxuries – but a necessity.' But one room to themselves was enough. She did not believe that they needed arm chairs to sit in or pictures to look at. She herself lived austerely in lodgings till she was seventy-two, combative, argumentative, frankly preferring a labour meeting at Venice to the pictures and the palaces, consumed with an abstract passion for justice to women which burnt up trivial personalities and made her a little intolerant of social frivolities. Was it worth while, she once asked, in her admirable, caustic manner, after meeting Lady Augusta Stanley, to go among the aristocracy? 'I felt directly that if I went to Lady

Stanley's again, I must get a new bonnet. And is it well to spend one's money in bonnets and flys instead of on instructive books?' she wondered. For Miss Davies perhaps was a little deficient in feminine charm.

That was a charge that nobody could bring against Lady Augusta Stanley. No two women could on the surface have less in common. Lady Augusta, it is true, was no more highly educated in a bookish sense than the middle-class women whom Miss Davies championed. But she was the finest flower of the education which for some centuries the little class of aristocratic women had enjoyed. She had been trained in her mother's drawing-room in Paris. She had talked to all the distinguished men and women of her time – Lamartine, Mérimée, Victor Hugo, the Duc de Broglie, Sainte-Beuve, Renan, Jenny Lind, Turgenev – everybody came to talk to old Lady Elgin and to be entertained by her daughters. There she developed that abounding sensibility, that unquenchable sympathy which were to be so lavishly drawn upon in after years. For she was very young when she entered the Duchess of Kent's household. For fifteen years of her youth she lived there. For fifteen years she was the life and soul of that 'quiet affectionate dull household of old people at Frogmore and Clarence House'. Nothing whatever happened. They drove out and she thought how charming the village children looked. They walked and the Duchess picked heather. They came home and the Duchess was tired. Yet not for a moment, pouring her heart out in profuse letters to her sisters, does she complain or wish for any other existence.

Seen through her peculiar magnifying glass, the slightest event in the life of the Royal family was either harrowing in the extreme or beyond words delightful. Prince Arthur was more handsome than ever. The Princess Helena was

so lovely. Princess Ada fell from her pony. Prince Leo was
naughty. The Beloved Duchess wanted a green umbrella.
The measles had come out, but, alas, they threatened to go
in again. One might suppose, to listen to Lady Augusta
exclaiming and protesting in alternate rapture and despair,
that to read aloud to the old Duchess of Kent was the most
exciting of occupations, and that the old ladies' rheumatisms
and headaches were catastrophes of the first order. For
inevitably the power of sympathy when so highly developed
and discharged solely upon personal relations tends to
produce a hothouse atmosphere in which domestic details
assume prodigious proportions and the mind feeds upon
every detail of death and disease with a gluttonous relish.
The space devoted in this volume to illness and marriage
entirely outweighs any reference to art, literature or politics.
It is all personal, emotional, and detailed as one of the
novels which were written so inevitably by women.

It was such a life as this and such an atmosphere as this
that Mr Greg and the *Saturday Review* and many men who
had themselves enjoyed the utmost rigours of education
wished to see preserved. And perhaps there was some excuse
for them. It is difficult to be sure, after all, that a college
don is the highest type of humanity known to us; and there
is something in Lady Augusta's power to magnify the
common and illumine the dull which seems to imply a very
arduous education of some sort behind it. Nevertheless, as
one studies the lives of the two women side by side, one
cannot doubt that Miss Davies got more interest, more
pleasure, and more use out of one month of her life than
Lady Augusta out of a whole year of hers. Some inkling
of the fact seems to have reached Lady Augusta even at
Windsor Castle. Perhaps being a woman of the old type is
a little exhausting; perhaps it is not altogether satisfying.

Lady Augusta at any rate seems to have got wind of other possibilities. She liked the society of literary people best, she said. 'I had always said that I had wished to be a fellow of a college,' she added surprisingly. At any rate she was one of the first to support Miss Davies in her demand for a University education for women. Did Miss Davies then sacrifice her book and buy her bonnet? Did the two women, so different in every other way, come together over this – the education of their sex? It is tempting to think so, and to imagine sprung from that union of the middle-class woman and the court lady some astonishing phoenix of the future who shall combine the new efficiency with the old amenity, the courage of the indomitable Miss Davies and Lady Augusta's charm.

Why?

When the first number of *Lysistrata* appeared, I confess that
I was deeply disappointed. It was so well printed, on such
good paper. It looked established, prosperous. As I turned
the pages it seemed to me that wealth must have descended
upon Somerville, and I was about to answer the request of
the editor for an article with a negative, when I read, greatly
to my relief, that one of the writers was badly dressed, and
gathered from another that the women's colleges still lack
power and prestige. At this I plucked up heart, and a crowd
of questions that have been pressing to be asked rushed to
my lips saying: Here is our chance.

I should explain that like so many people nowadays I
am pestered with questions. I find it impossible to walk
down the street without stopping, it may be in the middle
of the road, to ask Why? Churches, public houses, parliaments, shops, loud-speakers, motor cars, the drone of an
aeroplane in the clouds, and men and women, all inspire
questions. Yet what is the point of asking questions of
oneself? They should be asked openly in public. But the
great obstacle to asking questions openly in public is, of
course, wealth. The little twisted sign that comes at the
end of a question has a way of making the rich writhe;
power and prestige come down upon it with all their weight.
Questions, therefore, being sensitive, impulsive, and often

foolish, have a way of picking their asking place with care. They shrivel up in an atmosphere of power, prosperity, and timeworn stone. They die by the dozen on the threshold of great newspaper offices. They slink away to less favoured, less flourishing quarters where people are poor and therefore have nothing to give, where they have no power and therefore have nothing to lose. Now the questions that have been pestering me to ask them decided, whether rightly or wrongly, that they could be asked in *Lysistrata*. They said, 'We do not expect you to ask us in ——' here they named some of our most respectable dailies and weeklies; 'nor in ——' here they named some of our most venerable institutions. 'But, thank Heaven!' they exclaimed, 'are not women's colleges poor and young? Are they not inventive, adventurous? Are they not out to create a new ——'

'The editor forbids feminism,' I interposed severely.

'What is feminism?' they screamed with one accord, and as I did not answer at once, a new question was flung at me, 'Don't you think it high time that a new ——?' But I stopped them by reminding them that they had only two thousand words at their disposal, upon which they consulted together, and finally put forward the request that I should introduce one or two of the simplest, tamest, and most obvious among them. For example, there is the question that always bobs up at the beginning of term when societies issue their invitations and universities open their doors – why lecture, why be lectured?

In order to place this question fairly before you, I will describe, for memory has kept the picture bright, one of those rare but, as Queen Victoria would have put it, never-to-be-sufficiently-lamented occasions when in deference to friendship, or in a desperate attempt to acquire information about, perhaps, the French Revolution, it seemed necessary to attend a lecture. The room to begin with had a hybrid look – it was not for sitting in, nor yet for eating in. Perhaps there was a map on the wall; certainly there was a table on a platform, and several rows of rather small, rather hard, comfortless little chairs. These were occupied intermittently, as if they shunned each other's company, by people of both sexes, and some had notebooks and were tapping their fountain pens, and some had none and gazed with the vacancy and placidity of bull frogs at the ceiling. A large clock displayed its cheerless face, and when the hour struck in strode a harried-looking man, a man from whose face nervousness, vanity, or perhaps the depressing and impossible nature of his task had removed all traces of ordinary humanity. There was a momentary stir. He had written a book, and for a moment it is interesting to see people who have written books. Everybody gazed at him. He was bald and not hairy; had a mouth and a chin; in short he was a man like another, although he had written a book. He cleared his throat and the lecture began. Now, the human voice is an instrument of varied power; it can enchant and it can soothe; it can rage and it can despair; but when it lectures it almost always bores. What he said was sensible enough; there was learning in it and argument and reason; but as the voice went on attention wandered. The face of the clock seemed abnormally pale; the hands too suffered from some infirmity. Had they the gout? Were they swollen? They moved so slowly. They reminded one of the painful progress of a three-legged fly that has survived the winter. How many flies on an average survive the English winter, and what would be the thoughts of such an insect on waking to find itself being lectured on the French Revolution? The enquiry was fatal. A link had been lost – a paragraph dropped. It was useless to ask the lecturer to repeat his words; on he plodded with dogged pertinacity. The origin of the French Revolution was being sought for – also the thoughts of flies. Now there came one of those flat stretches of discourse when minute objects can be seen coming for two or three miles ahead. 'Skip!' we entreated him – vainly. He did not skip. He went on. Then there was a joke; then it seemed that the windows wanted washing; then a woman sneezed; then the voice quickened; then there was a peroration; and then – thank Heaven! the lecture was over.

Why, since life holds only so many hours, waste one of them on being lectured? Why, since printing presses have been invented these many centuries, should he not have printed his lecture instead of speaking it? Then, by the fire in winter, or under an apple tree in summer, it could have been read, thought over, discussed; the difficult ideas pondered, the argument debated. It could have been thickened, and stiffened. There would have been no need of those repetitions and dilutions with which lectures have to be watered down and brightened up so as to attract the attention of a miscellaneous audience too apt to think about noses and chins, women sneezing and the longevity of flies.

It may be, I told these questions, that there is some reason, imperceptible to outsiders, which makes lectures an essential part of university discipline. But why – here another rushed to the forefront – why, if lectures are necessary as a form of education should they not be abolished as a form of entertainment? Never does the crocus flower or the beech tree redden but there issues simultaneously from all the universities of England, Scotland and Ireland a shower of notes in which desperate secretaries entreat So-and-so and So-and-so to come down and address them upon art or literature, or politics, or morality – and why?

In the old days, when newspapers were scarce and

carefully lent about from Hall to Rectory, such laboured methods of rubbing up minds and imparting ideas were no doubt essential. But now, when every day of the week scatters our tables with articles and pamphlets in which every shade of opinion is expressed, far more tersely than by word of mouth, why continue an obsolete custom which not merely wastes time and temper, but incites the most debased of human passions – vanity, ostentation, self-assertion, and the desire to convert? Why encourage your elders to turn themselves into prigs and prophets, when they are ordinary men and women? Why force them to stand on a platform for forty minutes while you reflect upon the colour of their hair and the longevity of flies? Why not let them talk to you and listen to you, naturally and happily, on the floor? Why not create a new form of society founded on poverty and equality? Why not bring together people of all ages and both sexes of all shades of fame and obscurity so that they can talk, without mounting platforms, or reading papers, or wearing expensive clothes, or eating expensive food? Would not such a society be worth, even as a form of education, all the papers on art and literature that have ever been read since the world began? Why not abolish prigs and prophets? Why not invent human intercourse? Why not try?

Here, being sick of the word 'why', I was about to indulge myself with a few reflections of a general nature upon society as it was, as it is, as it might be, with some fancy pictures of Mrs Thrale entertaining Dr Johnson, of Lady Holland amusing Lord Macaulay thrown in, when such a clamour arose among the questions that I could hardly hear myself think. The cause of the clamour was soon apparent. I had incautiously and foolishly used the word 'literature'. Now if there is one word that excites questions and puts them in a fury it is this word 'literature'. There they were, screaming and crying, asking questions about poetry and fiction and criticism, each demanding to be heard, each certain that his was the only question that deserved an answer. At last, when they had destroyed all my fancy pictures of Lady Holland and Dr Johnson, one insisted, for he said that foolish and rash as he might be he was less so than the others, that he should be asked. And his question was, why learn English literature at universities when you can read it for yourselves in books? But I said it is foolish to ask a question that has already been answered – English literature is, I believe, already taught at the universities. Besides, if we are going to start an argument about it, we should need at least twenty volumes, whereas we have only about seven hundred words left to us. Still, as he was importunate, I said I would ask the question and introduce it to the best of my ability, without expressing any opinion of my own, by copying down the following fragment of dialogue.

The other day I went to call upon a friend of mine who earns her living as a publisher's reader. The room was a little dark it seemed to me when I went in. Yet, as the window was open and it was a fine spring day, the darkness must have been spiritual – the effect of some private sorrow I feared. Her first words as I came in confirmed my fears. 'Alas, poor boy!' she exclaimed, tossing the manuscript she was reading to the ground, with a gesture of despair.

Had some accident happened to one of her relations, I asked, motoring or climbing?

'If you call three hundred pages on the evolution of the Elizabethan sonnet an accident,' she said.

'Is that all?' I replied with relief.

'All?' she retaliated. 'Isn't it enough?' And, beginning to

pace up and down the room, she exclaimed, 'Once he was a clever boy; once he was worth talking to; once he cared about English literature. But now –' She threw out her hands as if words failed her – but not at all. There followed such a flood of lamentation and vituperation – but reflecting how hard her life was, reading manuscripts day in and day out, I excused her – that I could not follow the argument. All I could gather was that this lecturing about English literature – 'If you want to teach them to read English,' she threw in, 'teach them to read Greek' – all this passing of examinations in English literature, which led to all this writing about English literature, was sure in the end to be the death and burial of English literature. 'The tombstone,' she was proceeding, 'will be a bound volume of –' when I stopped her and told her not to talk such nonsense. 'Then tell me,' she said, standing over me with her fists clenched, 'Do they write any better for it? is poetry better, is fiction better, is criticism better, now that they have been taught how to read English literature?'

As if to answer her own question she read a passage from the manuscript on the floor. 'And each the spit and image of the other!' she groaned, lifting it wearily to its place with the manuscripts on the shelf.

'But think of all they must know?' I tried to argue. 'Know?' she echoed me. 'Know? What d'you mean by "know"?' As that was a difficult question to answer offhand, I passed it over by saying, 'Well, at any rate, they'll be able to make their livings and teach other people.' Whereupon she lost her temper and, seizing the unfortunate work upon the Elizabethan sonnet, whizzed it across the room. The rest of the visit passed in picking up the fragments of a vase that had belonged to her grandmother.

Now, of course, a dozen other questions clamour to be

asked; about Churches and Parliaments and public houses and shops and loud-speakers and men and women; but mercifully time is up; silence falls.

The Leaning Tower

A writer is a person who sits at a desk and keeps his eye fixed, as intently as he can, upon a certain object – that figure of speech may help to keep us steady on our path if we look at it for a moment. He is an artist who sits with a sheet of paper in front of him trying to copy what he sees. What is his object – his model? Nothing so simple as a painter's model; it is not a bowl of flowers, a naked figure, or a dish of apples and onions. Even the simplest story deals with more than one person, with more than one time. Characters begin young; they grow old; they move from scene to scene, from place to place. A writer has to keep his eye upon a model that moves, that changes, upon an object that is not one object but innumerable objects. Two words alone cover all that a writer looks at – they are, human life.

Let us look at the writer next. What do we see – only a person who sits with a pen in his hand in front of a sheet of paper? That tells us little or nothing. And we know very little. Considering how much we talk about writers, how much they talk about themselves, it is odd how little we know about them. Why are they so common sometimes; then so rare? Why do they sometimes write nothing but masterpieces, then nothing but trash? And why should a family, like the Shelleys, like the Keatses, like the Brontës, suddenly burst into flame and bring to birth Shelley, Keats, and the Brontës? What are the conditions that bring about that explosion? There is no answer – naturally. Since we have not yet discovered the germ of influenza, how should we yet have discovered the germ of genius? We know even less about the mind than about the body. We have less evidence. It is less than two hundred years since people took an interest in themselves; Boswell was almost the first writer who thought that a man's life was worth writing a book about. Until we have more facts, more biographies, more autobiographies, we cannot know much about ordinary people, let alone about extraordinary people. Thus at present we have only theories about writers – a great many theories, but they all differ. The politician says that a writer is the product of the society in which he lives, as a screw is the product of a screw machine; the artist, that a writer is a heavenly apparition that slides across the sky, grazes the earth and vanishes. To the psychologists a writer is an oyster; feed him on gritty facts, irritate him with ugliness and by way of compensation, as they call it, he will produce a pearl. The genealogists say that certain stocks, certain families, breed writers as fig trees breed figs – Dryden, Swift and Pope they tell us were all cousins. This proves that we are in the dark about writers; anybody can make a theory; the germ of a theory is almost always the wish to prove what the theorist wishes to believe.

Theories then are dangerous things. All the same we must risk making one this afternoon since we are going to discuss modern tendencies. Directly we speak of tendencies or movements we commit ourselves to the belief that there is some force, influence, outer pressure which is strong enough to stamp itself upon a whole group of different writers so that all their writing has a certain common likeness. We must then have a theory as to what this influence is. But let us always remember – influences are infinitely numerous; writers are infinitely sensitive; each writer has a different sensibility. That is why literature is always changing, like the weather, like the clouds in the sky. Read a page of Scott; then of Henry James; try to work out the influences that have transformed the one page into the other. It is beyond our skill. We can only hope therefore to single out the most obvious influences that have formed writers into groups. Yet there are groups. Books descend from books as families descend from families. Some descend from Jane Austen; others from Dickens. They resemble their parents, as human children resemble their parents; yet they differ as children differ, and revolt as children revolt. Perhaps it will be easier to understand living writers as we take a quick look at some of their forebears. We have not time to go far back – certainly we have not time to look closely. But let us glance at English writers as they were a hundred years ago – that may help us to see what we ourselves look like.

In 1815 England was at war, as England is now. And it is natural to ask, how did their war – the Napoleonic war – affect them? Was that one of the influences that formed them into groups? The answer is a very strange one. The Napoleonic wars did not affect the great majority of those writers at all. The proof of that is to be found in the work of two great novelists – Jane Austen and Walter Scott. Each lived through the Napoleonic wars; each wrote through them. But, though novelists live very close to the life of their time, neither of them in all their novels mentioned the Napoleonic wars. This shows that their model, their vision of human life, was not disturbed or agitated or changed by war. Nor were they themselves. It is easy to see why that was so. Wars were then remote; wars were carried on by soldiers and sailors, not by private people. The rumour of battles took a long time to reach England. It was only when the mail coaches clattered along the country roads hung with laurels that the people in villages like Brighton knew that a victory had been won and lit their candles and stuck them in their windows. Compare that with our state today. Today we hear the gunfire in the Channel. We turn on the wireless; we hear an airman telling us how this very afternoon he shot down a raider; his machine caught fire; he plunged into the sea; the light turned green and then black; he rose to the top and was rescued by a trawler. Scott never saw the sailors drowning at Trafalgar; Jane Austen never heard the cannon roar at Waterloo. Neither of them heard Napoleon's voice as we hear Hitler's voice as we sit at home of an evening.

That immunity from war lasted all through the nineteenth century. England, of course, was often at war – there was the Crimean War; the Indian Mutiny; all the little Indian frontier wars, and at the end of the century the Boer War. Keats, Shelley, Byron, Dickens, Thackeray, Carlyle, Ruskin, the Brontës, George Eliot, Trollope, the Brownings – all lived through all those wars. But did they ever mention them? Only Thackeray I think; in *Vanity Fair* he described the Battle of Waterloo long after it was fought; but only as an illustration, as a scene. It did not change his characters' lives; it merely killed one of his heroes. Of the poets only Byron and Shelley felt the influence of the nineteenth-century wars profoundly.

War then we can say, speaking roughly, did not affect either the writer or his vision of human life in the nineteenth century. But peace – let us consider the influence of peace. Were the nineteenth-century writers affected by the settled, the peaceful and prosperous state of England? Let us collect a few facts before we launch out into the dangers and delights of theory. We know for a fact, from their lives, that the nineteenth-century writers were all of them fairly well-to-do middle-class people. Most had been educated either at Oxford or at Cambridge. Some were civil servants like Trollope and Matthew Arnold. Others, like Ruskin, were professors. It is a fact that their work brought them considerable fortunes. There is visible proof of that in the houses they built. Look at Abbotsford, bought out of the proceeds of Scott's novels; or at Farringford, built by Tennyson from his poetry. Look at Dickens' great house in Marylebone; and at his great house at Gadshill. All these are houses needing many butlers, maids, gardeners, grooms to keep the tables spread, the cans carried, and the gardens neat and fruitful. Not only did they leave behind them large houses; they left too an immense body of literature – poems, plays, novels, essays, histories, criticism. It was a very prolific, creative, rich century – the nineteenth century. Now let us ask – is there any connection between that material prosperity and that intellectual creativeness? Did one lead to the other? How difficult it is to say – for we know so little about writers, and what conditions help them, what hinder them. It is only a guess, and a rough guess; yet I think that there is a connection. 'I think' – perhaps it would be nearer the truth to say 'I see.' Thinking should be based on facts; and here we have intuitions rather than facts – the lights and shades that come after books are read, the general shifting surface of a large expanse of print. What I see, glancing over that shifting surface, is the picture I have already shown you; the writer seated in front of human life in the nineteenth century; and, looking at it through their eyes, I see that life divided up, herded together, into many different classes.

There is the aristocracy; the landed gentry; the professional class; the commercial class; the working class; and there, in one dark blot, is that great class which is called simply and comprehensively 'The Poor'. To the nineteenth-century writer human life must have looked like a landscape cut up into separate fields. In each field was gathered a different group of people. Each to some extent had its own traditions; its own manners; its own speech; its own dress; its own occupation. But owing to that peace, to that prosperity each group was tethered, stationary – a herd grazing within its own hedges. And the nineteenth-century writer did not seek to change those divisions; he accepted them. He accepted them so completely that he became unconscious of them. Does that serve to explain why it is that the nineteenth-century writers are able to create so many characters who are not types but individuals? Is it because he did not see the hedges that divide classes; he saw only the human beings that live within those hedges? Is that why he could get beneath the surface and create many-sided characters – Pecksniff, Becky Sharp, Mr Woodhouse – who change with the years, as the living change? To us now the hedges are visible. We can see now that each of those writers only dealt with a very small section of human life – all Thackeray's characters are upper middle-class people; all Dickens' characters come from the lower or middle class. We can see that now; but the writer himself seems unconscious that he is only dealing with one type; with the type formed by the class into which the writer was born himself, with which he is most familiar. And that unconsciousness was an immense advantage to him.

Unconsciousness, which means presumably that the under-mind works at top speed while the upper mind drowses, is a state we all know. We all have experience of the work done by unconsciousness in our own daily lives. You have had a crowded day, let us suppose, sightseeing in London. Could you say what you had seen and done when you came back? Was it not all a blur, a confusion? But after what seemed a rest, a chance to turn aside and look at something different, the sights and sounds and sayings that had been of most interest to you swam to the surface, apparently of their own accord; and remained in memory; what was unimportant sank into forgetfulness. So it is with the writer. After a hard day's work, trudging round, seeing all he can, feeling all he can, taking in the book of his mind innumerable notes, the writer becomes – if he can – unconscious. In fact, his under-mind works at top speed while his upper mind drowses. Then, after a pause the veil lifts; and there is the thing – the thing he wants to write about – simplified, composed. Do we strain Wordsworth's famous saying about emotion recollected in tranquillity when we infer that by tranquillity he meant that the writer needs to become unconscious before he can create?

If we want to risk a theory, then, we can say that peace and prosperity were influences that gave the nineteenth-century writers a family likeness. They had leisure; they had security; life was not going to change; they themselves were not going to change. They could look; and look away. They could forget; and then – in their books – remember. Those then are some of the conditions that brought about a certain family likeness, in spite of the great individual differences, among the nineteenth-century writers. The nineteenth century ended; but the same conditions went on. They lasted, roughly speaking, till the year 1914. Even in 1914 we can still see the writer sitting as he sat all through the nineteenth century looking at human life; and that human life is still divided into classes; he still looks most intently at the class from which he himself springs; the classes are still so settled that he has almost forgotten that there are classes; and he is still so secure himself that he is almost unconscious of his own position and of its security. He believes that he is looking at the whole of life; and will always so look at it. That is not altogether a fancy picture. Many of those writers are still alive. Sometimes they describe their own position as young men, beginning to write, just before August 1914. How did you learn your art? One can ask them. At College they say – by reading; by listening; by talking. What did they talk about? Here is Mr Desmond MacCarthy's answer, as he gave it, a week or two ago, in the *Sunday Times*. He was at Cambridge just before the war began and he says: 'We were not very much interested in politics. Abstract speculation was much more absorbing; philosophy was more interesting to us than public causes. . . . What we chiefly discussed were those "goods" which were ends in themselves . . . the search for truth, aesthetic emotions, and personal relations.' In addition they read an immense amount; Latin and Greek, and of course French and English. They wrote too – but they were in no hurry to publish. They travelled; – some of them went far afield – to India, to the South Seas. But for the most part they rambled happily in the long summer holidays through England, through France, through Italy. And now and then they published books – books like Rupert Brooke's poems; novels like E. M. Forster's *Room with a View*; essays like G. K. Chesterton's essays, and reviews. It seemed to them that they were to go on living like that, and writing like that, for ever and ever. Then suddenly, like a chasm in a smooth road, the war came.

But before we go on with the story of what happened after 1914, let us look more closely for a moment, not at the writer himself, nor at his model; but at his chair. A chair is a very important part of a writer's outfit. It is the chair that gives him his attitude towards his model; that decides what he sees of human life; that profoundly affects his power of telling us what he sees. By his chair we mean his upbringing, his education. It is a fact, not a theory, that all writers from Chaucer to the present day, with so few exceptions that one hand can count them, have sat upon the same kind of chair – a raised chair. They have all come from the middle class; they have had good, at least expensive, educations. They have all been raised above the mass of people upon a tower of stucco – that is their middle-class birth; and of gold – that is their expensive education. That was true of all the nineteenth-century writers, save Dickens; it was true of all the 1914 writers, save D. H. Lawrence. Let us run through what are called 'representative names': G. K. Chesterton; T. S. Eliot; Belloc; Lytton Strachey; Somerset Maugham; Hugh Walpole; Wilfred Owen; Rupert Brooke; J. E. Flecker; E. M. Forster; Aldous Huxley; G. M. Trevelyan; O. and S. Sitwell; Middleton Murry. Those are some of them; and all, with the exception of D. H. Lawrence, came of the middle class, and were educated at public schools and universities. There is another fact, equally indisputable: the books that they wrote were among the best books written between 1910 and 1925. Now let us ask, is there any connection between those facts? Is there a connection between the excellence of their work and the fact that they came of families rich enough to send them to public schools and universities?

Must we not decide, greatly though those writers differ, and shallow as we admit our knowledge of influences to be, that there must be a connection between their education and their work? It cannot be a mere chance that this minute class of educated people had produced so much that is good as writing; and that the vast mass of people without education has produced so little that is good. It is a fact, however. Take away all that the working class has given to English literature and that literature would scarcely suffer; take away all that the educated class has given, and English literature would scarcely exist. Education must then play a very important part in a writer's work.

That seems so obvious that it is astonishing how little stress has been laid upon the writer's education. It is perhaps because a writer's education is so much less definite than other educations. Reading, listening, talking, travel, leisure – many different things it seems are mixed together. Life and books must be shaken and taken in the right proportions. A boy brought up alone in a library turns into a book worm; brought up alone in the fields he turns into an earth worm. To breed the kind of butterfly a writer is you must let him sun himself for three or four years at Oxford or Cambridge – so it seems. However it is done, it is there that it is done – there that he is taught his art. And he has to be taught his art. Again, is that strange? Nobody thinks it strange if you say that a painter has to be taught his art; or a musician; or an architect. Equally a writer has to be taught. For the art of writing is at least as difficult as the other arts. And though, perhaps because the education is indefinite, people ignore this education, if you look closely you will see that almost every writer who has practised his art successfully had been taught it. He had been taught it by about eleven years of education – at private schools, public schools and universities. He sits upon a tower raised above the rest of us; a tower built first on his parents' station, then on his parents' gold. It is a tower of the utmost importance; it decides his angle of vision; it affects his power of communication.

All through the nineteenth century, down to August 1914, that tower was a steady tower. The writer was scarcely conscious either of his high station, or of his limited vision. Many of them had sympathy, great sympathy, with other classes; they wished to help the working class to enjoy the advantages of the tower class; but they did not wish to destroy the tower, or to descend from it – rather to make it accessible to all. Nor had the model, human life, changed essentially since Trollope looked at it, since Hardy looked at it: and Henry James, in 1914, was still looking at it. Further, the tower itself held firm beneath the writer during all the most impressionable years, when he was learning his art, and receiving all those complex influences and instructions that are summed up by the word education. These were conditions that influenced their work profoundly. For when the crash came in 1914 all those young men, who were to be the representative writers of their time, had their past, their education, safe behind them, safe within them. They had known security; they had the memory of a peaceful boyhood, the knowledge of a settled civilisation. Even though the war cut into their lives, and ended some of them, they wrote, and still write, as if the tower were firm beneath them. In one word, they are aristocrats; the unconscious inheritors of a great tradition. Put a page of their writing under the magnifying-glass and you will see, far away in the distance, the Greeks, the Romans; coming nearer the Elizabethans; coming nearer still Dryden, Swift, Voltaire, Jane Austen, Dickens, Henry James. Each, however much he differs individually from the others, is a man of education; a man who has learnt his art.

From that group let us pass to the next – to the group which began to write about 1925 and, it may be, came to an end as a group in 1939. If you read current literary

journalism you will be able to rattle off a string of names
– Day Lewis, Auden, Spender, Isherwood, Louis MacNeice
and so on. They adhere much more closely than the names
of their predecessors. But at first sight there seems little
difference, in station, in education. Mr Auden in a poem
written to Mr Isherwood says: Behind us we have stucco
suburbs and expensive educations. They are tower dwellers
like their predecessors, the sons of well-to-do parents, who
could afford to send them to public schools and universities.
But what a difference in the tower itself, in what they saw
from the tower! When they looked at human life what did
they see? Everywhere change; everywhere revolution. In
Germany, in Russia, in Italy, in Spain, all the old hedges
were being rooted up; all the old towers were being thrown
to the ground. Other hedges were being planted; other
towers were being raised. There was communism in one
country; in another fascism. The whole of civilisation, of
society, was changing. There was, it is true, neither war
nor revolution in England itself. All those writers had time
to write many books before 1939. But even in England
towers that were built of gold and stucco were no longer
steady towers. They were leaning towers. The books were
written under the influence of change, under the threat of
war. That perhaps is why the names adhere so closely; there
was one influence that affected them all and made them,
more than their predecessors, into groups. And that
influence, let us remember, may well have excluded from
that string of names the poets whom posterity will value
most highly, either because they could not fall into step, as
leaders or as followers, or because the influence was adverse
to poetry, and until that influence relaxed, they could not
write. But the tendency that makes it possible for us to
group the names of these writers together, and gives their

work a common likeness, was the tendency of the tower they sat on – the tower of middle-class birth and expensive education – to lean.

Let us imagine, to bring this home to us, that we are actually upon a leaning tower and note our sensations. Let us see whether they correspond to the tendencies we observe in those poems, plays and novels. Directly we feel that a tower leans we become acutely conscious that we are upon a tower. All those writers too are acutely tower conscious; conscious of their middle-class birth; of their expensive educations. Then when we come to the top of the tower how strange the view looks – not altogether upside down, but slanting, sidelong. That too is characteristic of the leaning-tower writers; they do not look any class straight in the face; they look either up, or down, or sidelong. There is no class so settled that they can explore it unconsciously. That perhaps is why they create no characters. Then what do we feel next, raised in imagination on top of the tower? First discomfort; next self-pity for that discomfort; which pity soon turns to anger – to anger against the builder, against society, for making us uncomfortable. Those too seem to be tendencies of the leaning-tower writers. Discomfort; pity for themselves; anger against society. And yet – here is another tendency – how can you altogether abuse a society that is giving you after all a very fine view and some sort of security? You cannot abuse that society wholeheartedly while you continue to profit by that society. And so very naturally you abuse society in the person of some retired admiral or spinster or armament manufacturer; and by abusing them hope to escape whipping yourself. The bleat of the scapegoat sounds loud in their work, and the whimper of the schoolboy crying 'Please Sir it was the other fellow, not me.' Anger; pity; scapegoat beating; excuse finding – these are all very natural tendencies; if we were in their position we should tend to do the same. But we are not in their position; we have not had eleven years of expensive education. We have only been climbing an imaginary tower. We can cease to imagine. We can come down.

But they cannot. They cannot throw away their education; they cannot throw away their upbringing. Eleven years at school and college have been stamped upon them indelibly. And then, to their credit but to their confusion, the leaning tower not only leant in the thirties, but it leant more and more to the left. Do you remember what Mr MacCarthy said about his own group at the university in 1914? 'We were not very much interested in politics . . . philosophy was more interesting to us than public causes'? That shows that his tower leant neither to the right nor to the left. But in 1930 it was impossible – if you were young, sensitive, imaginative – not to be interested in politics; not to find public causes of much more pressing interest than philosophy. In 1930 young men at college were forced to be aware of what was happening in Russia; in Germany; in Italy; in Spain. They could not go on discussing aesthetic emotions and personal relations. They could not confine their reading to the poets; they had to read the politicians. They read Marx. They became communists; they became anti-fascists. The tower they realised was founded upon injustice and tyranny; it was wrong for a small class to possess an education that other people paid for; wrong to stand upon the gold that a bourgeois father had made from his bourgeois profession. It was wrong; yet how could they make it right? Their education could not be thrown away; as for their capital – did Dickens, did Tolstoy ever throw away their capital? Did D. H. Lawrence, a miner's son, continue to live like a miner? No; for it is death for a writer to throw away his capital; to be forced to earn his living in a mine or a factory. And thus, trapped by their education, pinned down by their capital, they remained on top of their leaning tower, and their state of mind as we see it reflected in their poems and plays and novels is full of discord and bitterness, full of confusion and of compromise.

These tendencies are better illustrated by quotation than by analysis. There is a poem, by one of those writers, Louis MacNeice, called *Autumn Journal*. It is dated March 1939. It is feeble as poetry, but interesting as autobiography. He begins of course with a snipe at the scapegoat – the bourgeois, middle-class family from which he sprang. The retired admirals, the retired generals, and the spinster lady have breakfasted off bacon and eggs served on a silver dish, he tells us. He sketches that family as if it were already a little remote and more than a little ridiculous. But they could afford to send him to Marlborough and then to Merton, Oxford. This is what he learnt at Oxford:

We learned that a gentleman never misplaces his accents,
That nobody knows how to speak, much less how to write
English who has not hob-nobbed with the great-grandparents
   of English.

Besides that he learnt at Oxford Latin and Greek; and philosophy, logic and metaphysics:

Oxford [he says] crowded the mantelpiece with gods –
Scaliger, Heinsius, Dindorf, Bentley, Wilamowitz.

It was at Oxford that the tower began to lean. He felt that he was living under a system –

That gives the few at fancy prices their fancy lives
While ninety-nine in the hundred who never attend the
    banquet
Must wash the grease of ages off the knives.

But at the same time, an Oxford education had made
him fastidious:

It is so hard to imagine
A world where the many would have their chance without
A fall in the standard of intellectual living
And nothing left that the highbrow cares about.

At Oxford he got his honours degree; and that degree
— in humane letters — put him in the way of a 'cushy job'
— seven hundred a year, to be precise, and several rooms
of his own.

If it were not for Lit. Hum. I might be climbing
A ladder with a hod
And seven hundred a year
Will pay the rent and the gas and the phone and the grocer —

And yet, again, doubts break in; the 'cushy job' of
teaching more Latin and Greek to more undergraduates
does not satisfy him —

. . . the so-called humane studies
May lead to cushy jobs
But leave the men who land them spiritually bankrupt,
Intellectual snobs.

And what is worse, that education and that cushy job

cut one off, he complains, from the common life of one's kind.

> All that I would like to be is human, having a share
> In a civilised, articulate and well-adjusted
> Community where the mind is given its due
> But the body is not distrusted.

Therefore, in order to bring about that well-adjusted community he must turn from literature to politics, remembering, he says,

> Remembering that those who by their habit
> Hate politics, can no longer keep their private
> Values unless they open the public gate
> To a better political system.

So, in one way or another, he takes part in politics, and finally he ends:

> What is it we want really?
> For what end and how?
> If it is something feasible, obtainable,
> Let us dream it now,
> And pray for a possible land
> Not of sleep-walkers, not of angry puppets,
> But where both heart and brain can understand
> The movements of our fellows
> Where life is a choice of instruments and none
> Is debarred his natural music . . .
> Where the individual, no longer squandered
> In self-assertion, works with the rest . . .

Those quotations give a fair description of the influences that have told upon the leaning-tower group. Others could easily be discovered. The influence of the films explains the lack of transitions in their work and the violently opposed contrasts. The influence of poets like Mr Yeats and Mr Eliot explains the obscurity. They took over from the elder poets a technique which, after many years of experiment, those poets used skilfully, and used it clumsily and often inappropriately. But we have time only to point to the most obvious influences; and these can be summed up as Leaning Tower Influences. If you think of them, that is, as people trapped on a leaning tower from which they cannot descend, much that is puzzling in their work is easier to understand. It explains the violence of their attack upon bourgeois society and also its half-heartedness. They are profiting by a society which they abuse. They are flogging a dead or dying horse because a living horse, if flogged, would kick them off its back. It explains the destructiveness of their work; and also its emptiness. They can destroy bourgeois society, in part at least; but what have they put in its place? How can a writer who has no first-hand experience of a towerless, of a classless society create that society? Yet as Mr MacNeice bears witness, they feel compelled to preach, if not by their living, at least by their writing, the creation of a society in which every one is equal and every one is free. It explains the pedagogic, the didactic, the loud speaker strain that dominates their poetry. They must teach; they must preach. Everything is a duty – even love. Listen to Mr Day Lewis ingeminating love. 'Mr. Spender,' he says, 'speaking from the living unit of himself and his friends appeals for the contraction of the social group to a size at which human contact may again be established and demands the destruction of all impediments to love. Listen.' And we listen to this:

We have come at last to a country
Where light, like shine from snow, strikes all faces
Here you may wonder
How it was that works, money, interest, building could
  ever
Hide the palpable and obvious love of man for man.

We listen to oratory not poetry. It is necessary, in order to feel the emotion of those lines, that other people should be listening too. We are in a group, in a class-room as we listen.

Listen now to Wordsworth:

Lover had he known in huts where poor men dwell
His daily teachers had been woods and rills,
The silence that is in the starry sky,
The sleep that is among the lonely hills

We listen to that when we are alone. We remember that in solitude. Is that the difference between politician's poetry and poet's poetry? We listen to the one in company; to the other when we are alone? But the poet in the thirties was forced to be a politician. That explains why the artist in the thirties was forced to be a scapegoat. If politics were 'real', the ivory tower was an escape from 'reality'. That explains the curious bastard language in which so much of this leaning-tower prose and poetry is written. It is not the rich speech of the aristocrat: it is not the racy speech of the peasant. It is betwixt and between. The poet is a dweller in two worlds, one dying, the other struggling to be born. And so we come to what is perhaps the most marked tendency of leaning-tower literature – the desire to be whole; to be human. 'All that I would like to be is human'

– that cry rings through their books – the longing to be closer to their kind, to write the common speech of their kind, to share the emotions of their kind, no longer to be isolated and exalted in solitary state upon their tower, but to be down on the ground with the mass of human kind.

These then, briefly and from a certain angle, are some of the tendencies of the modern writer who is seated upon a leaning tower. No other generation has been exposed to them. It may be that none has had such an appallingly difficult task. Who can wonder if they have been incapable of giving us great poems, great plays, great novels? They had nothing settled to look at; nothing peaceful to remember; nothing certain to come. During all the most impressionable years of their lives they were stung into consciousness – into self-consciousness, into class-consciousness, into the consciousness of things changing, of things falling, of death perhaps about to come. There was no tranquillity in which they could recollect. The inner mind was paralysed because the surface mind was always hard at work.

Yet if they have lacked the creative power of the poet and the novelist, the power – does it come from a fusion of the two minds, the upper and the under? – that creates characters that live, poems that we all remember, they have had a power which, if literature continues, may prove to be of great value in the future. They have been great egotists. That too was forced upon them by their circumstances. When everything is rocking round one, the only person who remains comparatively stable is oneself. When all faces are changing and obscured, the only face one can see clearly is one's own. So they wrote about themselves – in their plays, in their poems, in their novels. No other ten years can have produced so much autobiography as the ten years between 1930 and 1940. No one, whatever his class or his obscurity, seems to have reached the age of thirty without writing his autobiography. But the leaning-tower writers wrote about themselves honestly, therefore creatively. They told the unpleasant truths, not only the flattering truths. That is why their autobiography is so much better than their fiction or their poetry. Consider how difficult it is to tell the truth about oneself – the unpleasant truth; to admit that one is petty, vain, mean, frustrated, tortured, unfaithful, and unsuccessful. The nineteenth-century writers never told that kind of truth, and that is why so much of the nineteenth-century writing is worthless; why, for all their genius, Dickens and Thackeray seem so often to write about dolls and puppets, not about full-grown men and women; why they are forced to evade the main themes and make do with diversions instead. If you do not tell the truth about yourself you cannot tell it about other people. As the nineteenth century wore on, the writers knew that they were crippling themselves, diminishing their material, falsifying their object. 'We are condemned,' Stevenson wrote, 'to avoid half the life that passes us by. What books Dickens could have written had he been permitted! Think of Thackeray as unfettered as Flaubert or Balzac! What books I might have written myself? But they give us a little box of toys and say to us "You mustn't play with anything but these"!' Stevenson blamed society – bourgeois society was his scapegoat too. Why did he not blame himself? Why did he consent to go on playing with his little box of toys?

The leaning-tower writer has had the courage, at any rate, to throw that little box of toys out of the window. He has had the courage to tell the truth, the unpleasant truth, about himself. That is the first step towards telling the truth about other people. By analysing themselves honestly, with help from Dr Freud, these writers have done a great deal to free us from nineteenth-century suppressions. The writers of the next generation may inherit from them a whole state of mind, a mind no longer crippled, evasive, divided. They may inherit that unconsciousness which as we guessed – it is only a guess – at the beginning of this paper is necessary if writers are to get beneath the surface, and to write something that people remember when they are alone. For that great gift of unconsciousness the next generation will have to thank the creative and honest egotism of the leaning-tower group.

The next generation – there will be a next generation, in spite of this war and whatever it brings. Have we time then for a rapid glance, for a hurried guess at the next generation? The next generation will be, when peace comes, a post-war generation too. Must it too be a leaning-tower generation – an oblique, sidelong, self-centred, squinting, self-conscious generation with a foot in two worlds? Or will there be no more towers and no more classes and shall we stand, without hedges between us, on the common ground?

There are two reasons which lead us to think, perhaps to hope, that the world after the war will be a world without classes or towers. Every politician who has made a speech since September 1939 has ended with a peroration in which he has said that we are not fighting this war for conquest; but to bring about a new order in Europe. In that order, they tell us, we are all to have equal opportunities, equal chances of developing whatever gifts we may possess. That is one reason why, if they mean what they say, and can effect it, classes and towers will disappear. The other reason is given by the income tax. The income tax is already doing in its own way what the politicians are hoping to do in theirs. The income tax is saying to middle-class parents: You cannot afford to send your sons to public schools any longer; you must send them to the elementary schools. One of these parents wrote to the *New Statesman* a week or two ago. Her little boy, who was to have gone to Winchester, had been taken away from his elementary school and sent to the village school. 'He has never been happier in his life,' she wrote. 'The question of class does not arise; he is merely interested to find how many different kinds of people there are in the world. . . .' And she is only paying twopence-halfpenny a week for that happiness and instruction instead of 35 guineas a term and extras. If the pressure of the income tax continues, classes will disappear. There will be no more upper classes; middle classes; lower classes. All classes will be merged in one class. How will that change affect the writer who sits at his desk looking at human life? It will not be divided by hedges any more. Very likely that will be the end of the novel, as we know it. Literature, as we know it, is always ending, and beginning again. Remove the hedges from Jane Austen's world, from Trollope's world, and how much of their comedy and tragedy would remain? We shall regret our Jane Austens and our Trollopes; they gave us comedy, tragedy and beauty. But much of that old-class literature was very petty; very false; very dull. Much is already unreadable. The novel of a classless and towerless world should be a better novel than the old novel. The novelist will have more interesting people to describe – people who have had a chance to develop their humour, their gifts, their tastes; real people, not people cramped and squashed into featureless masses by hedges. The poet's gain is less obvious; for he has been less under the dominion of hedges. But he should gain words; when we have pooled all the different dialects, the clipped and cabined vocabulary which is all that he uses now should be enriched. Further, there might then be a common belief which he could accept, and thus shift from his shoulders the burden of didacticism, of propaganda. These then are a few reasons, hastily snatched, why we can look forward hopefully to a stronger, a more varied literature in the classless and towerless society of the future.

But it is in the future; and there is a deep gulf to be bridged between the dying world, and the world that is struggling to be born. For there are still two worlds, two separate worlds. 'I want,' said the mother who wrote to the paper the other day about her boy, 'the best of both worlds for my son.' She wanted, that is, the village school, where he learnt to mix with the living; and the other school – Winchester it was – where he mixed with the dead. 'Is he to continue,' she asked, 'under the system of free national education, or shall he go on – or should I say back – to the old public-school system which really is so very, very private?' She wanted the new world and the old world to unite, the world of the present and the world of the past.

But there is still a gulf between them, a dangerous gulf, in which, possibly, literature may crash and come to grief. It is easy to see that gulf; it is easy to lay the blame for it upon England. England has crammed a small aristocratic class with Latin and Greek and logic and metaphysics and mathematics until they cry out like the young men on the leaning tower, 'All that I would like to be is human.' She has left the other class, the immense class to which almost all of us must belong, to pick up what we can in village schools; in factories; in workshops; behind counters; and at home. When one thinks of that criminal injustice one is tempted to say England deserves to have no literature. She deserves to having nothing but detective stories, patriotic songs and leading articles for generals, admirals and business men to read themselves to sleep with when they are tired of winning battles and making money. But let us not be unfair; let us avoid if we can joining the embittered and futile tribe of scapegoat hunters. For some years now England has been making an effort – at last – to bridge the gulf between the two worlds. Here is one proof of that effort – this book. This book was not bought; it was not hired. It was borrowed from a public library. England lent it to a common reader, saying 'It is time that even you, whom I have shut out from all my universities for centuries, should learn to read your mother tongue. I will help you.' If England is going to help us, we must help her. But how? Look at what is written in the book she has lent us. 'Readers are requested to point out any defects that they may observe to the local librarian.' That is England's way of saying: 'If I lend you books, I expect you to make yourselves critics.'

We can help England very greatly to bridge the gulf between the two worlds if we borrow the books she lends us and if we read them critically. We have got to teach ourselves to understand literature. Money is no longer going to do our thinking for us. Wealth will no longer decide who shall be taught and who not. In future it is we who shall decide whom to send to public schools and universities; how they shall be taught; and whether what they write justifies their exemption from other work. In order to do that we must teach ourselves to distinguish – which is the book that is going to pay dividends of pleasure for ever; which is the book that will pay not a penny in two years' time? Try it for yourselves on new books as they come out; decide which are the lasting, which are the perishing. That is very difficult. Also we must become critics because in future we are not going to leave writing to be done for us by a small class of well-to-do young men who have only a pinch, a thimbleful of experience to give us. We are going to add our own experience, to make our own contribution. That is even more difficult. For that too we need to be critics. A writer, more than any other artist, needs to be a critic because words are so common, so familiar, that he must sieve them and sift them if they are to become enduring. Write daily; write freely; but let us always compare what we have written with what the great writers have written. It is humiliating, but it is essential. If we are going to preserve and to create, that is the only way. And we are going to do both. We need not wait till the end of the war. We can begin now. We can begin, practically and prosaically, by borrowing books from public libraries; by reading omnivorously, simultaneously, poems, plays, novels, histories, biographies, the old and the new. We must sample before we can select. It never does to be a nice feeder; each of us has an appetite that must find for itself the food that nourishes it. Nor let us shy away from the kings because we are commoners. That is a fatal crime in the eyes of Aeschylus, Shakespeare, Virgil, and Dante, who, if they could speak – and after all they can – would say, 'Don't leave me to the wigged and gowned. Read me, read me for yourselves.' They do not mind if we get our accents wrong, or have to read with a crib in front of us. Of course – are we not commoners, outsiders? – we shall trample many flowers and bruise much ancient grass. But let us bear in mind a piece of advice that an eminent Victorian who was also an eminent pedestrian once gave to walkers: 'Whenever you see a board up with "Trespassers will be prosecuted," trespass at once.'

Let us trespass at once. Literature is no one's private ground; literature is common ground. It is not cut up into nations; there are no wars there. Let us trespass freely and fearlessly and find our own way for ourselves. It is thus that English literature will survive this war and cross the gulf — if commoners and outsiders like ourselves make that country our own country, if we teach ourselves how to read and how to write, how to preserve and how to create.

Places

Peacehaven

Would it much affect us, we ask ourselves, if a sea monster erected his horrid head off the coast of Sussex and licked up the entire population of Peacehaven and then sank to the bottom of the sea? Should we mourn them, or wish for their resurrection? No; for none of the qualities for which we love our kind and respect its misfortunes are here revealed; all for which we despise it and suspect it are here displayed. All that is cheap and greedy and meretricious, that is to say, has here come to the surface, and lies like a sore, expressed in gimcrack red houses and raw roads and mean-ingless decorations and 'constant hot water' and 'inside sanitation' and 'superb views of the sea'. We did not know that we had so much evil in us. Here shown up against the background of nature we can weigh it to the last ounce. The road has been turned into a switchback; the cliff into a 'park' for motor-cars. Human beings bask inside them, dipping alternately into paper bags for peppermints and into newspapers for comic cuts, while the sea and the downs perform for them the same function that the band performs when they eat ices at Lyons's. Compared with this, Wembley is beautiful, and the Mile End Road respectable, while, when we cut loose at last and turn into open country, we feel inclined to worship the first flock of sheep that we meet and venerate the simplest of shepherds.

America, which I Have Never Seen . . .

'What interests you most in this cosmopolitan world of today?'

That is an enormous question; the world is a very large object, buzzing and humming on every inch of its surface with interesting things. But if we compress and epitomise, this essence and abstract of the world and its interesting things reduces itself undoubtedly to the United States of America. *America is the most interesting thing in the world today*.

But what – if, like me, you have never been to America – does America mean to you? What does it look like, and the Americans themselves – what are they like?

These are questions that the English, marooned on their island, are always asking of Imagination. And Imagination, unfortunately, is not an altogether accurate reporter; but she has her merits: she travels fast; she travels far. And she is obliging. When the question was put to her the other day, 'What is America like?' she gave her wings a shake and said, in her lighthearted way: 'Sit still on a rock on the coast of Cornwall; and I will fly to America and tell you what America is like.' So saying, she was off.

'I have passed fishing boats,' she began, 'tramp steamers; the *Queen Mary*; several airplanes. The sea looks much like any other sea; there is now a shoal of porpoises cutting cart wheels beneath me.

'But what is that huge grey rock? It appears to be the figure of a giant woman who seems, as I come closer, to be lighted up, whether with electric light or with the light of reason I am not at this moment certain. Behold! It is the Statue of Liberty. Liberty introducing America!

'Liberty seems clothed in radiant silver. The air here is about a thousand times clearer than the air in England. There is not a shred of mist or a wisp of fog; everything shines bright. The City of New York, over which I am now hovering, looks as if it had been scraped and scrubbed only the night before. It has no houses. It is made of immensely high towers, each pierced with a million holes.

'Coming closer, I see in every hole – they are windows – a typewriter and a desk. Down below in the streets long ribbons of traffic move steadily, on and on and on. Bells chime; lights flash. Everything is a thousand times quicker yet more orderly than in England. My mind feels speeded up. The blood courses through my veins. The old English words kick up their heels and frisk. A new language is coming to birth –'

'But look a little closer,' we interrupt – 'what strikes you about the houses in which people live?'

'That there is no privacy,' she resumed. 'The houses stand open to the road. No walls divide them; there are no gardens in front and no gardens behind. There are no curtains to the windows. You can see right in. The rooms are large and airy. There are no inglenooks or cosy corners. There are no old people drawn up over the fire, reading books. There is no fire.

'There are no dark family portraits hanging in shadowy recesses. Nor, although it is dinnertime, does a parlourmaid in cap and apron bring in a silver-covered dish. A spring is touched; a refrigerator opens; there is a whole meal ready to be eaten: clams on ice; ducks on ice; iced drinks in tall glasses; ice creams all colours of the rainbow.

'The Americans never sit down to a square meal. They perch on steel stools and take what they want from a perambulating rail. The Americans have swallowed their dinner by the time it takes us to decide whether the widow of a general takes precedence of the wife of a knight commander of the Star of India.

'When they have finished their meal the Americans, who are all in the prime of life, mostly clean-shaven if they are men, better built than we are, and extremely well groomed, both men and women, jump into their cars. Everyone has a car: the millionaire has one; the hired man has one; the hobo has one. And their cars go much more quickly than our cars, because the roads are as smooth as billiard balls and very straight. Sixty or seventy cars thus can drive abreast at the same time. Travelling at ninety miles an hour – but it feels like twenty – we are soon out of sight of houses. We are in the country.

'But the country is not like England, or Italy, or France. It is a primeval country: a country before there were countries. The space is vast; mountains rise; plains spread. Yet at some time, it is clear, people must have picnicked here in these woods; witness that heap of rusty tins; that deserted shed of corrugated iron; that skeleton of an old motorcar. But when the picnic was done they threw away the tins, the sheds, the cars, and on they drove! They never settled down and lived and died and were buried in the same spot.

'But now we are in the open again. Hold your hat to your head, for that giant man, standing as if he were carved in stone, makes one nervous, remembering *The Last of the Mohicans*, about one's scalp. He has a tomahawk in his hand, a blanket round his shoulders; eagle feathers ray out around his head. He is taking aim at some prehistoric extinct monster – surely that was a mammoth behind that rock?

'But next minute – remember the speed of the car – we are round the bend; we have dropped into a rich and fertile valley, willow-shaded, cow-pastured. From it mounts the mellow *lin-lan-lone* of church bells. Are we passing through some ancient English village on a Sunday morning? Is it May Day? Are they keeping up the ancient festival?

'The villagers are dancing round a Maypole; they are singing songs that have a strange familiar sound; we seem to have heard them before, in Shakespeare, in Herrick.

'This valley is like a cup into which time has dropped and stands clear and still. There is the England of Charles the First, still visible, still living in America. In her broad plains and deep valleys America has room for all ages, for all civilisations. There, just behind the corner, is the past – the red man aims his tomahawk at a bison; here in the car is the present; but what are we reaching now over the crest of the hill? Is it the future?

'For now we are running along the boulevards of an up-to-date city; the road is laid with blocks of concrete; the loud-speaker is ticking out the latest prices; druggists' stores are crowded with men in shirt sleeves; shop windows display complete outfits of Parisian clothes.

'But that immense building which might be a factory or a cathedral – what is that? It occupies a commanding position. In England it would be the King's palace. But here are no sentries; the doors stand open to all. The walls are made of stainless steel, the shelves of unbreakable glass. And there lie Shakespeare's folios, Ben Jonson's manuscripts,

Keats' love letters blazing in the light of the American sun.

'Down there in the courtyard is a palace lifted bodily from the Grand Canal; now we are in Stratford-upon-Avon; there is an Elizabethan cottage with the moss still growing on its tiles. From this extraordinary combination and collaboration of all cultures, of all civilisations will spring the future –'

'But,' we interrupt, 'tell us about the Americans in the present – the men and women. What are they like now, the inhabitants of this extraordinary land? Are they human beings as we are? Do they love and hate, sometimes feel tired, find it hard to get up in the morning, grumble at their wives?'

'The Americans themselves,' replies Imagination, 'are a most remarkable people. Superficially, they differ little from ourselves. That is to say, they wear petticoats and trousers; marry and bear children. But whether it is that the mountains are so high and may at any moment belch out fire and decimate a town, or that the rivers are so huge and may at any moment roll out their long liquid tongues and swallow up a city, or that the air is decidedly alcoholic so that everyone is always a little tipsy, the Americans are much freer, wilder, more generous, more adventurous, more spontaneous than we are.

'Look how they battle and punch; hack and hew; tunnel through mountains; erect skyscrapers; are ruined one moment, millionaires the next. In the same span of time we should have earned a modest pension, acquired a villa in Surrey, and decided, after due deliberation, to lop the cherry tree on the lawn.

'But the best way of illustrating the difference between them and us is to bid you observe that while we have shadows that stalk behind us, they have a light that dances in front of them. That is what makes them the most interesting people in the world – they face the future, not the past.'

So saying, Imagination folded her wings and settled on the Cornish rock again. While she had been to America and back, one old woman had filled her basket half full of dead sticks for her winter's firing. But of course, we must remember, Imagination, with all her merits, is not always strictly accurate.

Great Men's Houses

London, happily, is becoming full of great men's houses, bought for the nation and preserved entire with the chairs they sat on and the cups they drank from, their umbrellas and their chests of drawers. And it is no frivolous curiosity that sends us to Dickens's house and Johnson's house and Carlyle's house and Keats's house. We know them from their houses – it would seem to be a fact that writers stamp themselves upon their possessions more indelibly than other people. Of artistic taste they may have none; but they seem always to possess a much rarer and more interesting gift – a faculty for housing themselves appropriately, for making the table, the chair, the curtain, the carpet into their own image.

Take the Carlyles, for instance. One hour spent in 5 Cheyne Row will tell us more about them and their lives than we can learn from all the biographies. Go down into the kitchen. There, in two seconds, one is made acquainted with a fact that escaped the attention of Froude, and yet was of incalculable importance – they had no water laid on. Every drop that the Carlyles used – and they were Scots, fanatical in their cleanliness – had to be pumped by hand from a well in the kitchen. There is the well at this moment and the pump and the stone trough into which the cold water trickled. And here, too, is the wide and wasteful old grate upon which all kettles had to be boiled if they wanted a hot bath; and here is the cracked yellow tin bath, so deep and so narrow, which had to be filled with the cans of hot water that the maid first pumped and then boiled and then carried up three flights of stairs from the basement.

The high old house without water, without electric light, without gas fires, full of books and coal smoke and four-poster beds and mahogany cupboards, where two of the most nervous and exacting people of their time lived, year in year out, was served by one unfortunate maid. All through the mid-Victorian age the house was necessarily a battlefield where daily, summer and winter, mistress and maid fought against dirt and cold for cleanliness and warmth. The stairs, carved as they are and wide and dignified, seem worn by the feet of harassed women carrying tin cans. The high panelled rooms seem to echo with the sound of pumping and the swish of scrubbing. The voice of the house – and all houses have voices – is the voice of pumping and scrubbing, of coughing and groaning. Up in the attic under a skylight Carlyle groaned, as he wrestled with his history, on a horsehair chair, while a yellow shaft of London light fell upon his papers and the rattle of a barrel organ and the raucous shouts of street hawkers came through walls whose double thickness distorted but by no means excluded the sound. And the season of the house – for every house has its season – seems to be always the month of February, when cold and fog are in the street and torches flare and the rattle of wheels grows suddenly loud and dies away. February after February Mrs Carlyle lay coughing in the large four-poster hung with maroon curtains in which she was born, and as she coughed the many problems of the incessant battle, against dirt, against cold, came before her. The horsehair couch needed recovering; the drawing-room paper with its small, dark pattern needed cleaning; the yellow varnish on the panels was cracked and peeling – all must be stitched, cleansed, scoured with her own hands; and had she, or had she not, demolished the bugs that bred and bred in the ancient wood panelling? So the long watches of the sleepless night passed, and then she heard Mr Carlyle stir above her, and held her breath and wondered if Helen were up and had lit the fire and heated the water for his shaving. Another day had dawned and the pumping and the scrubbing must begin again.

Thus number 5 Cheyne Row is not so much a dwelling-place as a battlefield – the scene of labour, effort and perpetual struggle. Few of the spoils of life – its graces and its luxuries – survive to tell us that the battle was worth the effort. The relics of drawing-room and study are like the relics picked up on other battlefields. Here is a packet of old steel nibs; a broken clay pipe; a pen-holder such as schoolboys use; a few cups of white and gold china, much chipped; a horsehair sofa and a yellow tin bath. Here, too, is a cast of the thin worn hands that worked here; and of the excruciated and ravished face of Carlyle when his life was done and he lay dead here. Even the garden at the back of the house seems to be not a place of rest and recreation, but another smaller battlefield marked with a tombstone beneath which a dog lies buried. By pumping and by scrubbing, days of victory, evenings of peace and splendour were won, of course. Mrs Carlyle sat, as we see from the picture, in a fine silk dress, in a chair pulled up to a blazing fire and had everything seemly and solid about her; but at what cost had she won it! Her cheeks are hollow; bitterness and suffering mingle in the half-tender, half-tortured expression of the eyes. Such is the effect of a pump in the basement and a yellow tin bath up three pairs of stairs. Both husband and wife had genius; they loved each other; but what can genius and love avail against bugs and tin baths and pumps in the basement?

It is impossible not to believe that half their quarrels might have been spared and their lives immeasurably sweetened if only number 5 Cheyne Row had possessed, as the house agents put in, bath, h. and c., gas fires in the bedrooms, all modern conveniences and indoor sanitation. But then, we reflect, as we cross the worn threshold, Carlyle with hot water laid on would not have been Carlyle; and Mrs Carlyle without bugs to kill would have been a different woman from the one we know.

An age seems to separate the house in Chelsea where the Carlyles lived from the house in Hampstead which was shared by Keats and Brown and the Brawnes. If houses have their voices and places their seasons, it is always spring in Hampstead as it is always February in Cheyne Row. By some miracle, too, Hampstead has always remained not a suburb or a piece of antiquity engulfed in the modern world, but a place with a character peculiar to itself. It is not a place where one makes money, or goes when one has money to spend. The signs of discreet retirement are stamped on it. Its houses are neat boxes such as front the sea at Brighton with bow windows and balconies and deck chairs on verandahs. It has style and intention as if designed for people of modest income and some leisure who seek rest and recreation. Its prevailing colours are the pale pinks and blues that seem to harmonise with the blue sea and the white sand; and yet there is an urbanity in the style which proclaims the neighbourhood of a great city. Even in the twentieth century this serenity still pervades the suburb of Hampstead. Its bow windows still look out upon vales and trees and ponds and barking dogs and couples sauntering arm in arm and pausing, here on the hill-top, to look at the distant domes and pinnacles of London, as they sauntered and paused and looked when Keats lived here. For Keats lived up the lane in a little white house behind wooden palings. Nothing has been much changed since his day. But as we enter the house in which Keats lived some mournful shadow seems to fall across the garden. A tree has fallen and lies propped. Waving branches cast their shadows up and down over the flat white walls of the house. Here, for all the gaiety and serenity of the neighbourhood, the nightingale sang; here, if anywhere, fever and anguish had their dwelling and paced this little green plot oppressed with the sense of quick-coming death and the shortness of life and the passion of love and its misery.

Yet if Keats left any impress upon his house it is the impression not of fever, but of that clarity and dignity which come from order and self-control. The rooms are small but shapely; downstairs the long windows are so large that half the wall seems made of light. Two chairs turned together are close to the window as if someone had sat there reading and had just got up and left the room. The figure of the reader must have been splashed with shade and sun as the hanging leaves stirred in the breeze. Birds must have hopped close to his foot. The room is empty save for the two chairs, for Keats had few possessions, little furniture and not more, he said, than one hundred and fifty books. And perhaps it is because the rooms are so empty and furnished rather with light and shadow than with chairs and tables that one does not think of people, here where so many people have lived. The imagination does not evoke scenes. It does not strike one that there must have been eating and drinking here; people must have come in and out; they must have put down bags, left parcels; they must have scrubbed and cleaned and done battle with dirt and disorder and carried cans of water from the basement to the bedrooms. All the traffic of life is silenced. The voice of the house is the voice of leaves brushing in the wind; of branches stirring in the garden. Only one presence – that of Keats himself – dwells here. And even he, though his picture is on every wall, seems to come silently, on the broad shafts of light, without body or footfall. Here he sat on the chair in the window and listened without moving, and saw without starting, and turned the page without haste though his time was so short.

There is an air of heroic equanimity about the house in spite of the death masks and the brittle yellow wreaths and the other grisly memorials which remind us that Keats died young and unknown and in exile. Life goes on outside the window. Behind this calm, this rustling of leaves, one hears the far-off rattle of wheels, the bark of dogs fetching and carrying sticks from the pond. Life goes on outside the wooden paling. When we shut the gate upon the grass and the tree where the nightingale sang we find, quite rightly, the butcher delivering his meat from a small red motor van at the house next door. If we cross the road, taking care not to be cut down by some rash driver – for they drive at a great pace down these wide streets – we shall find ourselves on top of the hill and beneath shall see the whole of London lying below us. It is a view of perpetual fascination at all hours and in all seasons. One sees London as a whole – London crowded and ribbed and compact, with its dominant domes, its guardian cathedrals; its chimneys and spires; its cranes and gasometers; and the perpetual smoke which no spring or autumn ever blows away. London has lain there time out of mind scarring that stretch of earth deeper and deeper, making it more uneasy, lumped and tumultuous, branding it for ever with an indelible scar. There it lies in layers, in strata, bristling and billowing with rolls of smoke always caught on its pinnacles. And yet from Parliament Hill one can see, too, the country beyond. There are hills on the further side in whose woods birds are singing, and some stoat or rabbit pauses, in dead silence, with paw lifted to listen intently to rustlings among the leaves. To look over London from this hill Keats came and Coleridge and Shakespeare, perhaps. And here at this very moment the usual young man sits on an iron bench clasping to his arms the usual young woman.

Street Haunting:
A London Adventure

No one perhaps has ever felt passionately towards a lead pencil. But there are circumstances in which it can become supremely desirable to possess one; moments when we are set upon having an object, a purpose, an excuse for walking half across London between tea and dinner. As the foxhunter hunts in order to preserve the breed of horses, and the golfer plays in order that open spaces may be preserved from the builders, so when the desire comes upon us to go street rambling the pencil does for a pretext, and getting up we say, 'Really I must buy a pencil,' as if under cover of this excuse we could indulge safely in the greatest pleasure of town life in winter – rambling the streets of London.

The hour should be evening and the season winter, for in winter the champagne brightness of the air and the sociability of the streets are grateful. We are not then taunted as in summer by the longing for shade and solitude and sweet airs from the hayfields. The evening hour, too, gives us the irresponsibility which darkness and lamplight bestow. We are no longer quite ourselves. As we step out of the house on a fine evening between four and six we shed the self our friends know us by and become part of that vast republican army of anonymous trampers, whose society is

so agreeable after the solitude of one's own room. For there
we sit surrounded by objects which perpetually express the
oddity of our own temperaments and enforce the memories
of our own experience. That bowl on the mantelpiece, for
instance, was bought at Mantua on a windy day. We were
leaving the shop when the sinister old woman plucked at
our skirts and said she would find herself starving one of
these days, but 'Take it!' she cried, and thrust the blue and
white china bowl into our hands as if she never wanted to
be reminded of her quixotic generosity. So, guiltily, but
suspecting nevertheless how badly we had been fleeced, we
carried it back to the little hotel where, in the middle of
the night, the innkeeper quarrelled so violently with his
wife that we all leant out into the courtyard to look, and
saw the vines laced about among the pillars and the stars
white in the sky. The moment was stabilised, stamped like
a coin indelibly, among a million that slipped by imper-
ceptibly. There, too, was the melancholy Englishman, who
rose among the coffee cups and the little iron tables and
revealed the secrets of his soul – as travellers do. All this –
Italy, the windy morning, the vines laced about the pillars,
the Englishman and the secrets of his soul – rise up in a
cloud from the china bowl on the mantelpiece. And there,
as our eyes fall to the floor, is that brown stamp on the
carpet. Mr Lloyd George made that. 'The man's a devil!'
said Mr Cummings, putting the kettle down with which
he was about to fill the teapot so that it burnt a brown
ring on the carpet.

But when the door shuts on us, all that vanishes. The
shell-like covering which our souls have excreted to house
themselves, to make for themselves a shape distinct from
others, is broken, and there is left of all these wrinkles and
roughness a central oyster of perceptiveness, an enormous

eye. How beautiful a street is in winter! It is at once revealed and obscured. Here vaguely one can trace symmetrical straight avenues of doors and windows; here under the lamps are floating islands of pale light through which pass quickly bright men and women, who for all their poverty and shabbiness wear a certain look of unreality, an air of triumph, as if they had given life the slip, so that life, deceived of her prey, blunders on without them. But, after all, we are only gliding smoothly on the surface. The eye is not a miner, not a diver, not a seeker after buried treasure. It floats us smoothly down a stream, resting, pausing, the brain sleeps perhaps as it looks.

How beautiful a London street is then, with its islands of light, and its long groves of darkness, and on one side of it perhaps some tree-sprinkled, grass-grown space where night is folding herself to sleep naturally and, as one passes the iron railing, one hears those little cracklings and stirrings of leaf and twig which seem to suppose the silence of fields all round them, an owl hooting, and far away the rattle of a train in the valley. But this is London, we are reminded; high among the bare trees are hung oblong frames of reddish yellow light — windows; there are points of brilliance burning steady like low stars — lamps; this empty ground which holds the country in it and its peace is only a London square, set about by offices and houses where at this hour fierce lights burn over maps, over documents, over desks where clerks sit turning with wetted forefingers the files of endless corre-spondences; or more suffusedly the firelight wavers and the lamplight falls upon the privacy of some drawing-room, its easy chairs, its papers, its china, its inlaid table, and the figure of a woman, accurately measuring out the precise number of spoons of tea which — She looks at the door as if she heard a ring downstairs and somebody asking, is she in?

But here we must stop peremptorily. We are in danger of digging deeper than the eye approves; we are impeding our passage down the smooth stream by catching at some branch or root. At any moment, the sleeping army may stir itself and wake in us a thousand violins and trumpets in response; the army of human beings may rouse itself and assert all its oddities and sufferings and sordidities. Let us dally a little longer, be content still with surfaces only – the glossy brilliance of the motor omnibuses; the carnal splendour of the butchers' shops with their yellow flanks and their purple streaks; the blue and red bunches of flowers burning so bravely through the plate glass of the florists' windows.

For the eye has this strange property: it rests only on beauty; like a butterfly it seeks out colour and basks in warmth. On a winter's night like this, when Nature has been at pains to polish and preen itself, it brings back the prettiest trophies, breaks off little lumps of emerald and coral as if the whole earth were made of precious stone. The thing it cannot do (one is speaking of the average unprofessional eye) is to compose these trophies in such a way as to bring out their more obscure angles and relation-ships. Hence after a prolonged diet of this simple, sugary fare, of beauty pure and uncomposed, we become conscious of satiety. We halt at the door of the boot shop and make some little excuse, which has nothing to do with the real reason for folding up the bright paraphernalia of the streets and withdrawing to some duskier chamber of the being where we may ask, as we raise our left foot obediently upon the stand, 'What, then, is it like to be a dwarf?'

She came in escorted by two women who, being of normal size, looked like benevolent giants beside her. Smiling at the shop girls, they seemed to be at once disclaiming any lot in her deformity and assuring her of their protection. She wore the peevish yet apologetic expression usual on the faces of the deformed. She needed their kindness, yet she resented it. But when the shop girl has been summoned and the giantesses, smiling indulgently, had asked for shoes for 'this lady' and the girl had pushed the little stand in front of her, the dwarf stuck her foot out with an impetuosity which seemed to claim all our attention. Look at that! Look at that! she seemed to demand of us all, as she thrust her foot out, for behold it was the shapely, perfectly proportioned foot of a well-grown woman. It was arched; it was aristocratic. Her whole manner changed as she looked at it resting on the stand. She looked soothed and satisfied. Her manner became full of self-confidence. She sent for shoe after shoe; she tried on pair after pair. She got up and pirouetted before a glass which reflected the foot only in yellow shoes, in fawn shoes, in shoes of lizard skin. She raised her little skirts and displayed her little legs. She was thinking that, after all, feet are the most important part of the whole person; women, she said to herself, have been loved for their feet alone. Seeing nothing but her feet, she imagined perhaps that the rest of her body was of a piece with those beautiful feet. She was shabbily dressed, but she was ready to lavish any money upon her shoes. And as this was the only occasion upon which she was not afraid of being looked at but positively craved attention, she was ready to use any device to prolong the choosing and fitting. Look at my feet, look at my feet, she seemed to be saying, as she took a step this way and then a step that way. The shop girl good-humouredly must have said something flattering, for suddenly her face lit up in an ecstasy. But, after all, the giantesses, benevolent though they were, had their own affairs to see to; she must make up her mind; she must decide which to choose. At length, the pair was chosen and, as she walked out between her guardians, with the parcel swinging from her finger, the ecstasy faded, knowledge returned, the old peevishness, the old apology came back, and by the time she had reached the street again she had become a dwarf.

But she had changed the mood; she had called into being an atmosphere which, as we followed her out into the street, seemed actually to create the humped, the twisted, the deformed. Two bearded men, brothers apparently, stone-blind, supporting themselves by resting a hand on the head of a small boy between them, marched down the street. On they came with the unyielding yet tremulous tread of the blind, which seems to lend to their approach something of the terror and inevitability of the fate that has overtaken them. As they passed, holding straight on, the little convoy seemed to cleave asunder the passers-by with the momentum of its silence, its directness, its disaster. Indeed, the dwarf had started a hobbling grotesque dance to which everybody in the street now conformed: the stout lady tightly swathed in shiny sealskin; the feeble-minded boy sucking the silver knob of his stick; the old man squatted on a doorstep as if, suddenly overcome by the absurdity of the human spectacle, he had sat down to look at it – all joined in the hobble and tap of the dwarf's dance.

In what crevices and crannies, one might ask, did they lodge, this maimed company of the halt and the blind? Here, perhaps, in the top rooms of these narrow old houses between Holborn and the Strand, where people have such queer names, and pursue so many curious trades, are gold beaters, accordion pleaters, cover buttons, or others who support life, with even greater fantasticality, upon a traffic in cups with saucers, china umbrella handles, and highly coloured pictures of martyred saints. There they lodge, and it seems as if the lady in the sealskin jacket must find life tolerable, passing the time of day with the accordion pleater, or the man who covers buttons; life which is so fantastic cannot be altogether tragic. They do not grudge us, we are musing, our prosperity; when, suddenly, turning the corner, we come upon a bearded Jew, wild, hunger-bitten, glaring out of his misery; or pass the humped body of an old woman flung abandoned on the step of a public building with a cloak over her like the hasty covering thrown over a dead horse or donkey. At such sights, the nerves of the spine seem to stand erect; a sudden flare is brandished in our eyes; a question is asked which is never answered. Often enough these derelicts choose to lie not a stone's throw from theatres, within hearing of barrel organs, almost, as night draws on, within touch of the sequined cloaks and bright legs of diners and dancers. They lie close to those shop windows where commerce offers to a world of old women laid on doorsteps, of blind men, of hobbling dwarfs, sofas which are supported by the gilt necks of proud swans; tables inlaid with baskets of many coloured fruit, sideboards paved with green marble the better to support the weight of boars' heads, gilt baskets, candelabra; and carpets so softened with age that their carnations have almost vanished in a pale green sea.

Passing, glimpsing, everything seems accidentally but miraculously sprinkled with beauty, as if the tide of trade which deposits its burden so punctually and prosaically upon the shores of Oxford Street had this night cast up nothing but treasure. With no thought of buying, the eye is sportive and generous; it creates; it adorns; it enhances. Standing out in the street, one may build up all the chambers of a vast imaginary house and furnish them at one's will with sofa, table, carpet. That rug will do for the hall. That alabaster bowl shall stand on a carved table in the window. Our merrymakings shall be reflected in that thick round mirror. But, having built and furnished the house one is happily under no obligation to possess it; one can dismantle it in the twinkling of an eye, build and furnish another house with other chairs and other glasses. Or let us indulge ourselves at the antique jewellers, among the trays of rings and the hanging necklaces. Let us choose those pearls, for example, and then imagine how, if we put them on, life would be changed. It becomes instantly between two and three in the morning; the lamps are burning very white in the deserted streets of Mayfair. Only motor cars are abroad at this hour, and one has a sense of emptiness, of airiness, of secluded gaiety. Wearing pearls, wearing silk, one steps out on to a balcony which overlooks the gardens of sleeping Mayfair. There are a few lights in the bedrooms of great peers returned from Court, of silk-stockinged footmen, of dowagers who have pressed the hands of statesmen. A cat creeps along the garden wall. Love-making is going on sibilantly, seductively in the darker places of the room behind thick green curtains. Strolling sedately as if he were promenading a terrace beneath which the shires and counties of England lie sun-bathed, the aged Prime Minister recounts to Lady So-and-So with the curls and the emeralds the true history of some great crisis in the affairs of the land. We seem to be riding on the top of the highest mast of the tallest ship; and yet at the same time we know that nothing of this sort matters, love is not proved thus, nor great achievements completed thus; so that we sport with the moment and preen our feathers in it lightly, as we stand on the balcony watching the moonlit cat creep along Princess Mary's garden wall.

But what could be more absurd? It is, in fact, on the stroke of six; it is a winter's evening; we are walking to the Strand to buy a pencil. How then are we also on a balcony, wearing pearls in June? What could be more absurd? Yet it is Nature's folly, not ours. When she set about her chief masterpiece, the making of man, she should have thought of one thing only. Instead, turning her head, looking over her shoulder, into each one of us she let creep instincts and desires which are utterly at variance with his main being, so that we are streaked, variegated, all of a mixture; the colours have run. Is the true self this which stands on the pavement in January, or that which bends over the balcony in June? Am I here, or am I there? Or is the true self neither this nor that, neither here nor there, but something so varied and wandering that it is only when we give the rein to its wishes and let it take its way unimpeded that we are indeed ourselves? Circumstances compel unity; for convenience' sake a man must be a whole. The good citizen when he opens his door in the evening must be banker, golfer, husband, father; not a nomad wandering the desert, a mystic staring at the sky, a debauchee in the slums of San Francisco, a soldier heading a revolution, a pariah howling with scepticism and solitude. When he opens his door, he must run his fingers through his hair and put his umbrella in the stand like the rest.

But here, none too soon, are the second-hand bookshops. Here we find anchorage in these thwarting currents of being; here we balance ourselves after the splendours and miseries of the streets. The very sight of the bookseller's wife with her foot on the fender, sitting beside a good coal fire, screened from the door, is sobering and cheerful. She is never reading, or has only the newspaper; her talk when it leaves bookselling, as it does so gladly, is about hats; she likes a hat to be practical, she says, as well as pretty. Oh no, they don't live at the shop; they live at Brixton; she must have a bit of green to look at. In summer a jar of flowers grown in her own garden is stood on the top of some dusty pile to enliven the shop. Books are everywhere; and always the same sense of adventure fills us. Second-hand books are wild books, homeless books; they have come together in vast flocks of variegated feather, and have a charm which the domesticated volumes of the library lack. Besides, in this random, miscellaneous company we may rub against some complete stranger who will, with luck, turn into the best friend we have in the world. There is always a hope, as we reach down some greyish-white book from an upper shelf, directed by its air of shabbiness and desertion, of meeting here with a man who set out on horseback over a hundred years ago to explore the woollen market in the midlands and Wales; an unknown traveller, who stayed at inns, drank his pint, noted pretty girls and serious customs, wrote it all down stiffly, laboriously for sheer love of it (the book was published at his own expense); was infinitely prosy, busy, and matter-of-fact, and so let flow in without his knowing it the very scent of the hollyhocks and the hay together with such a portrait of himself as gives him forever a seat in the warm corner of the mind's inglenook. One may buy him for eighteen pence now. He is marked three and sixpence, but the bookseller's wife, seeing how shabby the covers are and how long the book has stood there since it was bought at some sale of a gentleman's library in Suffolk, will let it go at that.

Thus, glancing round the bookshop, we make other such sudden capricious friendships with the unknown and the vanished whose only record is, for example, this little book of poems, so fairly printed, so finely engraved, too, with a portrait of the author. For he was a poet and drowned untimely, and his verse, mild as it is and formal and sententious, sends forth still a frail fluty sound like that of a piano organ played in some back street resignedly by an old Italian organ-grinder in a corduroy jacket. There are travellers, too, row upon row of them, still testifying, indomitable spinsters that they were, to the discomforts that they endured and the sunsets they admired in Greece when Queen Victoria was a girl; a tour in Cornwall with a visit to the tin mines was thought worthy of voluminous record; people went slowly up the Rhine and did portraits of each other in Indian ink, sitting reading on deck beside a coil of rope; they measured the pyramids; were lost to civilisation for years; converted negroes in pestilential swamps. This packing up and going off, exploring deserts and catching fevers, settling in India for a lifetime, penetrating even to China and then returning to lead a parochial life at Edmonton, tumbles and tosses upon the dusty floor like an uneasy sea, so restless the English are, with the waves at their very door. The waters of travel and adventure seem to break upon little islands of serious effort and lifelong industry stood in jagged column upon the bookshop floor. In these piles of puce-bound volumes with gilt monograms on the back, thoughtful clergymen expound the gospels; scholars are to be heard with their hammers and their chisels chipping clear the ancient texts of Euripides and Aeschylus. Thinking, annotating, expounding, goes on at a prodigious rate all round us and over everything, like a punctual, everlasting tide, washes the ancient sea of fiction. Innumerable volumes tell how Arthur loved Laura and they were separated and they were unhappy and then they met and they were happy ever after, as was the way when Victoria ruled these islands.

The number of books in the world is infinite, and one is forced to glimpse and nod and go on after a moment of talk, a flash of understanding, as, in the street outside, one catches a word in passing and from a chance phrase fabricates a lifetime. It is about a woman called Kate that they are talking, how 'I said to her, quite straight last night . . . if you don't think I'm worth a penny stamp, I said . . .' But who Kate is, and to what crisis in their friendship the penny stamp refers, we shall never know; for Kate sinks under the warmth of their volubility; and here, at the street corner, another page of the volume of life is laid open by the sight of two men consulting under the lamp post. They are spelling out the latest wire from Newmarket in the stop press news. Do they think, then, that fortune will ever convert their rags into fur and broad-cloth, sling them with watch chains, and plant diamond pins where there is now a ragged open shirt? But the main stream of walkers at this hour sweeps too fast to let us ask such questions. They are wrapt, in this short passage from work to home, in some narcotic dream, now that they are free from the desk, and have the fresh air on their cheeks. They put on those bright clothes which they must hang up and lock the key upon all the rest of the day, and are great cricketers, famous actresses, soldiers who have saved their country at the hour of need. Dreaming, gesticulating, often muttering a few words aloud, they sweep over the Strand and across Waterloo Bridge whence they will be swung in long rattling trains, still dreaming, to some prim little villa in Barnes or Surbiton where the sight of the clock in the hall and the smell of the supper in the basement puncture the dream.

But we are come to the Strand now, and as we hesitate on the curb, a little rod about the length of one's finger begins to lay its bar across the velocity and abundance of life. 'Really I must – really I must' – that is it. Without investigating the demand, the mind cringes to the accustomed tyrant. One must, one always must, do something or other; it is not allowed one simply to enjoy oneself. Was it not for this reason that, some time ago, we fabricated that excuse, and invented the necessity of buying something? But what was it? Ah, we remember, it was a pencil. Let us go then and buy this pencil. But just as we are turning to obey the command, another self disputes the right of the tyrant to insist. The usual conflict comes about. Spread out behind the rod of duty we see the whole breadth of the River Thames – wide, mournful, peaceful. And we see it through the eyes of somebody who is leaning over the Embankment on a summer evening, without a care in the world. Let us put off buying the pencil; let us go in search of this person (and soon it becomes apparent that this person is ourselves). For if we could stand there where we stood six months ago, should we not be again as we were then – calm, aloof, content? Let us try then. But the river is rougher and greyer than we remembered. The tide is running out to sea. It brings down with it a tug and two barges, whose load of straw is tightly bound down beneath tarpaulin covers. There is too, close by us, a couple leaning over the balustrade murmuring with that curious lack of self-consciousness which lovers have, as if the importance of the affair they are engaged on claims without question the indulgence of the human race. The sights we see and the sounds we hear now have none of the quality of the past; nor have we any share in the serenity of the person who, six months ago, stood precisely where we stand now. His is the happiness of death; ours the insecurity of life. He has no future; the future is even now invading our peace. It is only when we look at the past and take from it the element of uncertainty that we can enjoy perfect peace. As it is, we must turn, we must cross the Strand again, we must find a shop where, even at this hour, they will be ready to sell us a pencil.

It is always an adventure to enter a new room; for the lives and characters of its owners have distilled their atmosphere into it, and directly we enter it we breast some new wave of emotion. Here, without a doubt, in the stationer's shop people had been quarrelling. Their anger shot through the air. They both stopped; the old woman – they were husband and wife evidently – retired to a back room; the old man whose rounded forehead and globular eyes would have looked well on the frontispiece of some Elizabethan folio, stayed to serve us. 'A pencil, a pencil,' he repeated, 'certainly, certainly.' He spoke with the distraction yet effusiveness of one whose emotions have been roused and checked in full flood. He began opening box after box and shutting them again. He said that it was very difficult to find things when they kept so many different articles. He launched into a story about some legal gentleman who had got into deep waters owing to the conduct of his wife. He had known him for years; he had been connected with the Temple for half a century, he said, as if he wished his wife in the back room to overhear him. He upset a box of rubber bands. At last, exasperated by his incompetence, he pushed the swing door open and called out roughly, 'Where d'you keep the pencils?' as if his wife had hidden them. The old lady came in. Looking at nobody, she put her hand with a fine air of righteous severity upon the right box. There were the pencils. How then could he do without her? Was she not indispensable to him? In order to keep them there, standing side by side in forced neutrality, one had to be particular in one's choice of pencils; this was too soft, that too hard. They stood silently looking on. The longer they stood there, the calmer they grew; their heat was going down, their anger disappearing. Now, without a word said on either side, the quarrel was made up. The old man who would not have disgraced Ben Jonson's title-page, reached the box back to its proper place, bowed profoundly his good night to us, and they disappeared. She would get out her sewing; he would read his newspaper; the canary would scatter them impartially with seed. The quarrel was over.

During these minutes in which a ghost had been sought for, a quarrel composed, and a pencil bought, the streets had become completely empty. Life had withdrawn to the top floor, and lamps were lit. The pavement was dry and hard; the road was of hammered silver. Walking home through the desolation one could tell oneself the story of the dwarf, of the blind men, of the party in the Mayfair mansion, of the quarrel in the stationer's shop. Into each of these lives one could penetrate a little way, far enough to give oneself the illusion that one is not tethered to a single mind but can put on briefly for a few minutes the bodies and minds of others. One could become a washerwoman, a publican, a street singer. And what greater delight and wonder can there be than to leave the straight lines of personality and deviate into those footpaths that lead beneath brambles and thick tree trunks into the heart of the forest where live those wild beasts, our fellow men?

That is true: to escape is the greatest of pleasures; street haunting in winter the greatest of adventures. Still as we approach our own doorstep again, it is comforting to feel the old possessions, the old prejudices, fold us round, and shelter and enclose the self which has been blown about at so many street corners, which has battered like a moth at

the flame of so many inaccessible lanterns. Here again is
the usual door; here the chair turned as we left it and the
china bowl and the brown ring on the carpet. And here –
let us examine it tenderly, let us touch it with reverence
– is the only spoil we have retrieved from the treasures of
the city, a lead pencil.

Notes

Virginia Woolf published two collections of her essays: *The Common Reader* (1925) and *The Common Reader: Second Series* (1932). Both are available in Vintage Classics, edited and annotated by Andrew McNeillie, and are abbreviated below as *CR1* and *CR2*.

The following notes are fairly basic, but a few will not be found elsewhere. Woolf's collected essays are fully annotated in *The Essays of Virginia Woolf*, six volumes edited by Andrew McNeillie (vols 1–4) and Stuart N. Clarke (vols 5–6), published by Random House under its Hogarth Press imprint. The texts of the essays in this book have been taken from these volumes, abbreviated as *E*1–6.

The Common Reader
This introductory essay was written especially for inclusion in *CR1*. Reprinted *E*4 p. 19.

The Anatomy of Fiction
A review (signed V. W.) in the *Athenaeum*, 16 May 1919, of *Materials and Methods of Fiction. Revised and Enlarged*, by Clayton Hamilton. Reprinted *E*3 pp. 43–7.

Wilcoxiana
A signed review in the *Athenaeum*, 19 September 1919, of

The Worlds and I, by Ella Wheeler Wilcox. Reprinted *E*3 pp. 97–102.

Trousers

An unsigned review in the *New Statesman*, 4 June 1921, of *The Things Which Are Seen*, by A. Trystan Edwards. Reprinted *E*3 pp. 312–14.

A Letter to a Lady in Paraguay

A signed article in the *Woman's Leader*, 5 May 1922. Reprinted *E*6 pp. 391–5.

Princess Bibesco was Elizabeth Charlotte Lucy (1897–1945), daughter of Herbert Henry Asquith (1852–1928), Prime Minister 1908–16, and his second wife, Margaret (Margot) Tennant (1864–1945); she had married the Romanian Prince Antoine Bibesco in 1919.

The Week End

An unsigned review in the *Times Literary Supplement*, 3 July 1924, of *The Week-End Book*, ed. Vera Mendel and Francis Meynell. Reprinted *E*3 pp. 414–16.

Miss Mitford

This essay in *CR1* is based on 'The Wrong Way of Reading' in the *Athenaeum*, 28 May 1920, and on 'An Imperfect Lady' in the *Times Literary Supplement*, 6 May 1920, two of three reviews of *Mary Russell Mitford and Her Surroundings*, by Constance Hill. Reprinted *E*4 pp. 190–5, and see pp. 208–9.

'Clara Butt: Her Life Story'

An unsigned review in the *Nation and Athenaeum*, 14 July 1928, of *Clara Butt: Her Life Story*, by Winifred Ponder, with

a foreword by Dame Clara Butt (1872–1936). Reprinted
*E*4 p. 551.

The Dream

A signed review in the *Listener*, 15 February 1940, of *Marie Corelli: The Life and Death of a Best-Seller*, by George Bullock. Reprinted *E*6 pp. 220–4.

Corelli's books, furniture, goods and personal possessions were sold off in October 1943. The University of Birmingham acquired Mason Croft after the war, and it now houses the University's Shakespeare Institute. There is a blue plaque to Corelli on the building.

The Royal Academy

A signed essay in the *Athenaeum*, 22 August 1919, on the Royal Academy's 151st Exhibition. Reprinted *E*3 pp. 89–95.

'for your sake, Alice': when she was young, Woolf read James Fennimore Cooper's novels. See his *The Pilot: A Tale of the Sea* (1824), ch. xiv: 'Not a hair of theirs shall be touched, not a thatch shall blaze, nor shall a sleepless night befall the vilest among them – and all for your sake, Alice!'

John Singer Sargent's *Gassed* (1919) was lent by the Imperial War Museum and was first shown in the RA Exhibition. A letter from Harry G. Sparks in the *Athenaeum*, 12 September 1919, stated that he had 'seen hundreds of [gassed] men do exactly the same thing' in France and that the 'over-emphasis' was 'on the part of the man – not on that of the artist'.

Roger Fry (1866–1934), leading art critic of the day and member of the Bloomsbury Group, was no admirer of the Royal Academy or of Sargent's paintings. In 'An Essay in Aesthetics' (1909), he wrote that a work of art should be considered as 'an expression of emotions considered as ends in themselves'. Woolf's biography of him is available in Vintage Classics.

Thunder at Wembley

A signed essay in the *Nation and the Athenaeum*, 28 June 1924, on the British Empire Exhibition, April–October 1924 (extended into 1925), which the Woolfs visited on 29 May. Reprinted *E*3 pp. 410–14.

In October 1924, Woolf commented on the weather of 'the deplorable summer that is dead' (*E*3 p. 449). In pre-decimal currency, six shillings and eightpence was exactly one-third of £1.

Middlebrow

A letter to the editor first published in *The Death of the Moth and Other Essays* (1942). Reprinted *E*6 pp. 470–79.

Footnote in *The Death of the Moth*: 'Keepaway is the name of a preparation used to distract the male dog from the female at certain seasons.'

Introductory Letter to Margaret Llewelyn Davies

This essay, originally published as 'Memories of a Working Women's Guild' in the *Yale Review*, September 1930, was revised as the introduction to *Life as We Have Known It* by Co-operative Working Women, ed. Margaret Llewelyn Davies (Hogarth Press, 1931). Reprinted *E*5 pp. 225–41, and see pp. 176–94.

Margaret Llewelyn Davies (1861–1944) was General Secretary of the Women's Co-operative Guild 1889–1922; Lilian Harris (d. 1949 or 1950) was Cashier of the Guild from 1893, Assistant Secretary 1902–21, and Davies' lifelong companion.

The Niece of an Earl

This essay, originally published in *Life and Letters*, October 1928, was slightly revised for inclusion in *CR2*. Reprinted *E*5 pp. 529–34, and see *E*4 pp. 559–63.

'radiant youth and august age waiting their summons within to be admitted to the presence of King George': George V reigned 1910–36. A young woman of good family was not considered to be an official member of Society until, accompanied by her sponsor, she had been presented to the monarch at Court; the custom was abolished in 1958.

Lady Dorothy Nevill

This essay, originally published as 'Behind the Bars' in the *Athenaeum*, 12 December 1919, as a review of *The Life and Letters of Lady Dorothy Nevill*, by Ralph Nevill, was very slightly revised for inclusion in *CR1*. Reprinted *E*4 pp. 200–4, and see pp. 208, 210–11.

'Queen Alexandra the Well-Beloved'

An unsigned review in the *Nation and the Athenaeum*, 6 February 1926, of *Queen Alexandra the Well-Beloved*, by Elizabeth Villiers. Reprinted *E*4 pp. 336–7.

Boy Jones: Edward Jones (1824–93) was a notorious intruder into Buckingham Palace between 1838 and 1841.

Royalty

An essay rejected by *Picture Post* in 1939 'as an attack on the Royal family, and on the institution of kingship in this country' and first published in *The Moment and Other Essays* (1947). Reprinted *E*6 pp. 504–9.

The 'little girls feeding the sea lions' and later 'feeding the panda' are Princesses Elizabeth (b. 1926, Queen Elizabeth II from 1952) and Margaret (1930–2002); the 'elderly lady accepting a bouquet' is Queen Mary (1867–1953), consort of George V. The 'old body in black with a pair of horn spectacles' is Queen Victoria (1819–1901, reigned from 1837). The heart that loved a Simpson belonged to Edward VIII (1894–1972), who abdicated on 11 December 1936 and was created Duke of Windsor; on 3 June 1937 he married Wallis Warfield (1895/6–1986), formerly Simpson, formerly Spencer, *née* Bessie Wallis Warfield of Baltimore. Simpson's department store, 203 Piccadilly, W1, opened in 1936. Queen Elizabeth, consort of George VI (1895–1952, reigned from 1936), *née* Bowes-Lyon (1900–2002), was the daughter of the 14th Earl of Strathmore and Kinghorne.

Dr Bentley

This essay on Dr Richard Bentley (1662–1742) was written especially for inclusion in *CR1*. Reprinted *E4* pp. 196–200, and see pp. 209–10.

'homunculus eruditione mediocri, ingenio nullo': a little man of middling learning and no ability.

'*equidem*': indeed.

'Et tunc [*i.e.* nunc] magna mei sub terris ibit imago': And now my great ghost will go under the earth.

Laetitia Pilkington

This essay, originally published in the *Nation and the Athenaeum*, 30 June 1923, was very slightly revised for inclusion in *CR1*. Reprinted *E4* pp. 127–31, and see pp. 141, 143–4.

Moll Flanders is the eponymous heroine of Defoe's novel of 1721. Anne Isabella Ritchie (1837–1919), novelist and memoirist, was the daughter of William Makepeace

Thackeray; her sister Harriet Marian ('Minnie') was the first wife of Woolf's father, Leslie Stephen.

Jones and Wilkinson
A signed essay in the *Bermondsey Book*, June 1926, based on *Memoirs of His Own Life* (4 vols, 1790), by Tate Wilkinson. Reprinted *E*4 pp. 354–9.

All About Books
A signed review in the *New Statesman and Nation*, 28 February 1931, and (with variations) in the *New Republic* (New York), 15 April, of *A Journal of My Journey to Paris in the Year 1765* . . ., by William Cole (1714–82), ed. Francis Griffin Stokes, with an introduction by Helen Waddell. Reprinted *E*5 pp. 219–25.

By Guess and by God, the 'very exciting yet infinitely childish book' by William Guy Carr, is subtitled *The Story of the British Submarines in the War*.

Woolf omits to mention that William Empson (1906–84) wrote about her in *Scrutinies*, compiled by Edgell Rickword. A 'bull's eye' was a lantern with a 'boss of glass, or the central protuberance formed in making a sheet of blown glass' (*OED*).

The Rev. William Cole: A Letter
A signed review in the *New Statesman and Nation*, 6 February 1932, of *The Blecheley Diary of the Rev. William Cole, M.A. F.S.A., 1765–67*, ed. Francis Griffin Stokes, with an introduction by Helen Waddell. Reprinted *E*5 pp. 289–94.

Archbishop Thomson
This essay, originally published as 'The Soul of an Archbishop'

in the *Athenaeum*, 9 May 1919, as a review of *The Life and Letters of William Thomson* [1819–90], *Archbishop of York*, by Ethel H. Thomson, was very slightly revised for inclusion in *CR1*. Reprinted *E4* pp. 204–8, and see pp. 211–12.

For more information about the Rev. John Purchas, see: www.saintpaulschurch.org.uk.

Miss Ormerod

This essay, originally published in the *Dial* (New York), December 1924, was based on *Eleanor Ormerod, LL.D. Economic Entomologist. Autobiography and Correspondence* (1904), ed. Robert Wallace, and was included in the first US edition of *CR1*. Reprinted *E6* pp. 647–55, and see pp. 636–7.

Two Women

A signed review in the *Nation and the Athenaeum*, 23 April 1927, of *Emily Davies and Girton College*, by Barbara Stephen, and of *Letters of Lady Augusta Stanley: A Young Lady at Court 1849–1863*, ed. the Dean of Windsor and Hector Bolitho. Reprinted *E4* pp. 419–26.

Why?

A signed essay in *Lysistrata*, May 1934, the second issue (it ran for five) of a magazine for the women's colleges of Oxford University. Reprinted *E6* pp. 30–36.

The Leaning Tower

A signed essay in *Folios of New Writing*, Autumn 1940, a biannual edited by John Lehmann and published by The Hogarth Press. The essay is based on a paper read on 27 April 1940 to the Workers' Educational Association in Brighton. Reprinted *E6* pp. 259–83.

The 'eminent Victorian' in the penultimate paragraph was Woolf's father Leslie Stephen (1832–1904), whose advice (expressed in different words) appears in his 1901 essay, 'In Praise of Walking'.

Peacehaven

An untitled paragraph in the 'Life and Letters' column signed 'Kappa' (S. K. Ratcliffe) in the *Nation and the Athenaeum*, 5 September 1925. It was introduced by 'A brilliant Englishwoman writes to me –'. Reprinted *E*4 p. 290.

Woolf repeats several well-worn estate agents' phrases, but it is interesting to turn to *The Times*, 23 March 1925, p. 1, col. d, halfway down the column of adverts, where near to one another there are references to 'superb views', 'inside sanitation' and 'constant hot water'.

America, which I Have Never Seen . . .

A signed essay in *Hearst's International combined with Cosmopolitan* (New York), April 1938. Reprinted *E*6 pp. 128–33.

Great Men's Houses

A signed essay in *Good Housekeeping*, March 1932, the third of six essays in a series called 'The London Scene'. Reprinted *E*5 pp. 294–301.

Charles Dickens's house at 48 Doughty St, WC1, was acquired by the Dickens Fellowship in 1925; Samuel Johnson's house at 17 Gough Square, EC4, was restored and opened to the public in 1912. The Carlyles' house at 24 (formerly 5) Cheyne Row, SW3, was transferred to the National Trust in 1936; all the items listed by Woolf can still be seen there, but the headstone that originally marked the grave of Mrs Carlyle's little dog Nero has unfortunately been removed. Keats lived with Charles Armitage Brown from 1818 to 1820 in what is now Keats Grove, Hampstead; there he fell in love with Fanny Brawne (1800–65) when she and her mother moved into the other half of the semi-detached house in 1819; the whole house was opened as a museum in 1925.

J. A. Froude (1818–94) was Carlyle's literary executor and published Carlyle's *Reminiscences* (1881), a four-volume biography of Carlyle (1882–4), Jane Welsh Carlyle's *Letters and Memorials* (1883) and *My Relations with Carlyle* (1903).

Street Haunting: A London Adventure

A signed essay in the *Yale Review*, October 1927, and published as a small book by the Westgate Press of San Francisco in 1930. Reprinted *E4* pp. 480–91; see also *E6* pp. 642–4.

It is not possible to map the narrator's walk accurately, but it seems to form a vertical oblong with the Woolfs' house, 52 Tavistock Square, in the top right-hand corner: from there, west to Tottenham Court Road, down Tottenham Court Road (well known for its furniture shops) into Charing Cross Road (famous for its bookshops), over to the Embankment, back up to the Strand, then towards home along Kingsway, Southampton Row and Upper Woburn Place.

'Princess Mary's garden wall': Princess Mary (1897–1965), only daughter of George V, and her husband Lord Lascelles (1882–1947) lived in Chesterfield House (demolished in 1937), on the corner of South Audley and Curzon Streets, Mayfair.

THE HISTORY OF VINTAGE

The famous American publisher Alfred A. Knopf (1892–1984) founded Vintage Books in the United States in 1954 as a paperback home for the authors published by his company. Vintage was launched in the United Kingdom in 1990 and works independently from the American imprint although both are part of the international publishing group, Random House.

Vintage in the United Kingdom was initially created to publish paperback editions of books bought by the prestigious literary hardback imprints in the Random House Group such as Jonathan Cape, Chatto & Windus, Hutchinson and later William Heinemann, Secker & Warburg and The Harvill Press. There are many Booker and Nobel Prize-winning authors on the Vintage list and the imprint publishes a huge variety of fiction and non-fiction. Over the years Vintage has expanded and the list now includes great authors of the past – who are published under the Vintage Classics imprint – as well as many of the most influential authors of the present. In 2012 Vintage Children's Classics was launched to include the much-loved authors of our youth.

For a full list of the books Vintage publishes,
please visit our website
www.vintage-books.co.uk

For book details and other information about the classic authors we publish, please visit the Vintage Classics website
www.vintage-classics.info